C000040774

Above The Stag Theatre presents

A HARD RAIN

by

Jon Bradfield and Martin Hooper

A Hard Rain was first performed at
Above the Stag Theatre, London, on 26 February 2014

A HARD RAIN

by Jon Bradfield and Martin Hooper

CAST in order of appearance

Nigel Barber	Frank, Army Official
Stephanie Willson	Angie
Michael Edwards	Ruby
Rhys Jennings	Danny
Oliver Lynes	Josh, Army Official
James El-Sharawy	Jimmy

Tricia Thorns	Director
David Shields	Designer
Elliot Griggs	Lighting Designer
Alexandra Bradford	Stage Manager

Peter Bull **for Above The Stag**	Producer

Cast and Creative Team

Nigel Barber | FRANK/ARMY OFFICIAL

Nigel trained at the Pacific Conservatory of the Performing Arts, Santa Maria, California; and the Stella Adler Academy of Acting and Theatre and the Actors Workshop (both in Los Angeles). His theatre in the UK includes: *The Bodyguard* (Adelphi Theatre, West End); *Hearts on Fire* (Nova C, Edinburgh); *The Drowsy Chaperone* (ROSS, Scarborough). Theatre in the USA includes: *After the Fall, The Gingerbread Lady, Stop the World I Want to Get Off* (Apollo Theatre, Los Angeles); *The Boys in the Band, Lenny, Pal Joey* (Off Broadway Theatre, San Diego); *The Physicists, Once Upon a Mattress, Barefoot Boy With Cheek, The Fantasticks* (La Jolla Repertory, San Diego); *The Boy Friend* (Old Globe, San Diego); *You're a Good Man Charlie Brown, Damn Yankees* (Golden Rolling Belly, Los Angeles). Theatre in Portugal includes: *Twelfth Night, Time of Your Life* (Teatro Lethes); *The Real Inspector Hound* (A Partado); *A Midsummer Night's Dream* (National Theatre). TV in the UK includes: *Parents, Seconds From Disaster – Jonestown, 50 Ways to Kill Your Lover, Aircrash Confidential 2, The Castaways*. TV in the USA includes: *Magnum PI, Harry O, Heaven Sent, Baywatch, Capital, The Hour of Saint Francis, Knight Rider, T.J. Hooker, The Young and the Restless*. Film includes: *The Partisan, The Sweeter Side of Life, Killing Oswald, The Underwater Realm, Project Artichoke, Remains, Melancholia, Obligate Symbiosis, Ashes to Ashes, Carpe Dium, A Distant Man, Bridge, Frozen Stars, Codex, Wheel of Fortune, Attack of the Killer Tomatoes, Happy Hour*.

Michael Edwards | RUBY

Trained at Drama Centre London. Theatre includes: *The Dog the Night and the Knife* (Arcola Theatre); *Flight* (Brockley Jack Theatre); *Jekyll and Hyde* (Southwark Playhouse); *House of Bones* (Platform Theatre); *The Last Days of Judas Iscariot* (Platform Theatre); *Michael Jackson at the Gates of Heaven and Hell* (Underbelly); *The Modern Mariner* (The Old Boys Club). Film includes: *Butterfly* (Wolfheart Productions); *Tiger House* (Strike Films); *Denousa* (Venetsano Films).

James El-Sharawy | JIMMY

James trained at Rose Bruford School of Theatre and Performance. Theatre includes: *Psychopomp and Circumstance* (Hen & Chickens); *Casualties of War* (Nightingale Theatre); *Poppy and the Plough, A Solider Dreams of White Tulips* (Paper Tiger at SOAS); *Tunnel* (Nightingale Theatre); *Portrait of a Man* (Promenade at Victoria and Albert Museum); *Qudz* (Yard Theatre); *Masked* (George Bernard Shaw Theatre, RADA); *Days of Significance* (Unicorn Theatre); *Death of a Salesman* (Rose Theatre); *Amir: The Lost Price of Persia* (Theatre503). Film includes: *Evidence of Existence* (Filmmaker at Large); *The Shotlist* (Josh Alward).

Oliver Lynes | JOSH/ARMY OFFICIAL

Oliver trained at the Bristol Old Vic Theatre School. Theatre includes: *Junket* (Miniaturists at Arcola Theatre); *James and the Giant Peach* (Birmingham Old Rep/UK national tour); *Merrily We Roll Along*, Volpone (Edinburgh Fringe); *Savages* (Royal Court Theatre – NYT). Theatre during training: *The Good Soul of Szechuan* (Bristol Old Vic Studio); *Macbeth* (Redgrave Theatre); *Hard Times* (Tobacco Factory). TV includes: *Life Out There* (BSLBT/Film4). Oliver was awarded The Actor's Centre's Alan Bates Runner-up Award 2012.

Rhys Jennings | DANNY

Rhys trained at the Royal Welsh College of Music and Drama. Theatre includes: *The Grumpiest Boy in the World* (Paper Balloon); *Humbug* (Theatre Clwyd); *DNA* (Hull Truck); *The Rivals* (Theatre Royal Bath/tour/West End); *Shhh, Auricular, Thatcherwrite* (Theatre503); *Newsrevue* (Canal Café Theatre); *The Sitcom Mission* (New Diorama); *Cymbeline* (Tabard Theatre); *The Night Porters* (Thistle Sifters). Rhys won the 2009 Carleton Hobbs Award and worked with the BBC Radio Drama Company for five months. Radio includes: *The Plantagenets, The Changeling* (dir. Jeremy Mortimer); *Black Hearts in Battersea, The Honourable Schoolboy* (dir. Marc Beeby); *Matilda* (dir. Claire Grove); *High-Lites, Planet B* (dir. Jessica Dromgoole). Rhys also voiced Captain Pascal in *Doctor Who: The Curse of Davros*, Dorian/Rory in *The Confessions of Dorian Gray* (Big Finish Productions), and is the voice of Jack Holden in computer game *Zombies, Run!*

Stephanie Willson | ANGIE

Stephanie trained at ArtsEd, London, and was a finalist in the Carleton Hobbs BBC Radio Awards. She appeared in *Jack Off the Beanstalk* for Above The Stag. Theatre includes: Summer Rep Season 2013 including *Don't Dress for Dinner, See How They Run, The Ghost Train, Blithe Spirit* (Sidmouth Manor Pavilion Theatre); *Whodunnit, Stepping Out* (Sidmouth and Greenwich Theatre); *Merlin the Magician, Romeo and Juliet, Love and Understanding* (all UK tours). She has performed at the Edinburgh Festival for the last five years including *Shakespeare for Breakfast*. Film includes: *Svengali, Before, After and After That*.

Jon Bradfield and Martin Hooper | Writers

Jon and Martin's pantomimes for Above The Stag include *Dick Whittington – Another Dick in City Hall; Robin Hood – Queen of Thieves; Sleeping Beauty – One Little Prick* (shortlisted Best Entertainment, Off West End Awards), *Get Aladdin!* and *Jack Off the Beanstalk*. Jon has also written for *NewsRevue* (Canal Café Theatre).

Peter Bull | Producer

Peter is artistic director of Above The Stag Theatre Company. He produced all the ATS in house productions in Victoria, notably *BLINK!, Dangerous, Boys Plays, The Choir, American Briefs, The Irish Curse, Bathhouse the Musical, Seduction, Busted Jesus Comix, Silence! The Musical, Maurice, My Beautiful Laundrette, Sleeping with Straight Men* and of course the annual Bradfield/Hooper panto mayhem. He also directed *American Briefs, Seduction* and *Extra Virgin* (the second half of *Boys Plays*). In the USA he has directed productions for the Players Theatre, New York, Spiral Theatre, Milwaukee and Bailiwick Repertory, Chicago as well as working with Mark Hooker on the infamous Milwaukee production of *Naked Boys Singing!* He was associate producer of *SHOUT! The Swinging 60's Musical* (Chicago/West End/UK tour).

Elliot Griggs | Lighting Designer

Elliot's lighting designs for Above The Stag include *Jack Off the Beanstalk* and *The Gay Naked Play*. Other theatre includes: *CommonWealth* (Almeida Theatre); *Fleabag* (Soho Theatre and tour); *The Boy Who Kicked Pigs* (The Lowry, Manchester/tour); *Over the Bridge, FACTS, Somersaults, The Soft of Her Palm, Crush, Perchance to Dream, Portraits, And I and Silence, Northern Star* (Finborough Theatre); *Belleville Rendez-Vous* (Greenwich Theatre); *MEAT* (Theatre503); *Lagan* (Ovalhouse); *Infanticide* (Camden People's Theatre); *Blues in the Night, Joe/Boy* (Last Refuge); *Love Re:Imagined* (Only Connect); *Folk Contraption* (Southbank Centre); *Bitter Pleasures for a Sour Generation* (Soho Theatre); *Big Sean, Mikey and Me* (Tristan Bates Theatre/Edinburgh Fringe Festival); *The Custard Boys* (Tabard

Theatre); *Dealing with Clair, One Minute, Nocturnal, dirty butterfly, Our Town* (Royal Academy of Dramatic Art); *The Mercy Seat* (RSC CAPITAL Centre, Warwick); *The Lady's Not for Burning, West Side Story, By the Bog of Cats, 'Tis Pity She's a Whore, Elephant's Graveyard* (Warwick Arts Centre); *Curious Directive's Drift: Photo 51* (Edinburgh Academy); *Much Ado About Nothing* (Belgrade Theatre); *Dido and Aeneas* (St Paul's Church, Covent Garden/tour). Awards include: the Francis Reid Award 2011, Association of Lighting Designers.

David Shields | Set and Costume Designer

David's previous designs for Above The Stag include *The Gay Naked Play, Jack Off the Beanstalk, Get Aladdin!* (ATS at the Landor Theatre), *Sleeping with Straight Men, Sleeping Beauty – One Little Prick, Boys Plays*. Other credits include: *The Snow Gorilla* (Rose Theatre Kingston); costumes for *The Busybody* (Southwark Playhouse); *The Sunny Side of the Street* (Jermyn Street Theatre); *Bash* (Barons Court); *One Flew Over the Cuckoo's Nest, Rent, Bare, Steel Pier* (various, London); *Little Shop of Horrors* (Aberystwyth); *Song & Dance, Carmen Jones* (European tours); *Oh! What a Night* (Blackpool Opera House); *A Christmas Carol* (Nottingham Theatre Royal); *Dick Whittington* (Bristol Hippodrome); Anthony Minghella's *Cigarettes and Chocolate, Lonely Hearts* (The Old Fire Station); *Money to Burn* (London); *Chess* 10th and 20th anniversary productions (Oslo Spektrum); *Dido and Aeneas* (Guildford); costumes for Jose Carreras' *Amore Perduto* (Dortmund); the Scandinavian productions of *Jesus Christ Superstar, Hair, Fame, Grease, Saturday Night Fever, Mannen Frå La Mancha* (Det Norske Teatret Oslo); *Mapp, Lucia* (London); *Naked Flame* and FRA winner of Best Farce, *Naked Flame – Fire Down Under* (UK tours); *The Hobbit* (Queens Theatre, London/UK tours); *Saturday Night Fever* (UK national tours/London/Madrid/Spanish tour); nine productions at the Royal Palace, Kirrwiller, France; also fifteen world-touring productions for Holiday on Ice. He also designed the set for *Strictly Come Dancing – The Professionals* tour; *Ice Age Live – A Mammoth Adventure* (Arena World Tour); and *Robin Cousins' Ice*.

Tricia Thorns | Director

Tricia began her career as an actress in the West End as part of John Neville's company at the Fortune, after a Classics BA from Nottingham University. As a director, her work includes: *What the Women Did – 2014 revival* (Southwark Playhouse); *London Wall* (Finborough Theatre/St James Theatre); *My Real War 1914–?* (Trafalgar Studios/national tour); *The Searcher* (Workshop production at Greenwich Theatre); *Red Night* (Finborough Theatre); *What the Women Did* (Southwark Playhouse); *Forgotten Voices from the Great War* (Pleasance London); *Ex, Black 'Ell* (Soho Theatre); *Twelfth Night* (Dulwich Picture Gallery); *Peer Gynt* (Alleyn's Theatre); *Passion Play 2000*, a huge community play which she also wrote. As an actress, theatre includes: *End of Story* (Chelsea Theatre); *Harry and Me* (Warehouse Theatre); *Façade* (Dingley and Dulwich Festivals); *A Kind of Alaska* (Edinburgh/tour/USA); *Time's Up* (Windsor); *The Libertine, The Man of Mode* (Royal Court/Out of Joint tour); *Betrayal* (BAC and tour); *Run for Your Wife* (West End); and leading roles in theatres in Salisbury, Ipswich, Edinburgh, Liverpool, Guildford, Derby and many more. Her many TV and film appearances include: *Dangerfield, A Touch of Frost, Keeping Up Appearances, The Darling Buds of May, The Bill, London's Burning, Captives, The Turn of the Screw*.

Above The Stag is London's only producing theatre with a focus on gay work. In November 2013, the theatre welcomed audiences for the first time to its new home venue in a renovated railway arch in Vauxhall with its most successful pantomime to date.

In its previous home, above the Stag pub in Victoria, Above The Stag was already one of London's most thriving fringe theatres. Its productions included seminal works such as *Maurice* and *My Beautiful Launderette*, new writing and discoveries from the US and Australia, original musicals and cabaret.

www.abovethestag.com
Arch 17, Miles Street, Vauxhall, London SW8 1RZ
Above The Stag is a Registered Charity No.1154069

A HARD RAIN

Jon Bradfield and Martin Hooper

Characters

ANGIE, *twenty-six to thirty*
FRANK, *forty to fifty-five*
RUBY, *male, twenty-six to thirty-five*
DANNY, *twenty-six*
JOSH, *twenty-two to twenty-six*
JIMMY, *sixteen*

ARMY OFFICIAL 1, *to be played by the actor playing Frank*
ARMY OFFICIAL 2, *to be played by the actor playing Josh*

Time and Place

Almost all of the action takes place in June, 1969, in Greenwich Village, New York City.

The opening scenes of Act Two are set in autumn 1968 on a military base in the United States.

Note

Ruby will always wear an element of drag, which may range from slightly feminised touches and a spot of make-up to full-on drag. The look would be slightly less polished and more improvised than we might expect of a drag performer today, though at times he could be equally flamboyant and eccentric.

This text went to press before the end of rehearsals and so may differ slightly from the play as performed.

ACT ONE

Dark. Violent sounds. Glass breaks, a door is broken in.
Shouting: some orders – 'Line up!' – someone is hurt, a chair is
broken, we hear handcuffs, somebody is hit. It crescendos and
blurs into a chaos. Then, silence, and lights up on...

Scene One

A bar, or soon to be. A very plain room with the walls mainly
painted black. At the front of the stage, the audience side, are
the 'windows' to the street, soon to be blacked out. Sunlight
floods in. An entrance downstage leads off to the entrance
lobby, coat check and the street. There is also an entrance
upstage, to the back room of the establishment. The bar itself is
pretty makeshift and little attempt has been made at decorating
the room, though a few posters are scattered on the floor
waiting to be hung on the walls. ANGIE and FRANK stick
some of these up during the scene. There are boxes of bottles to
be unpacked.

FRANK stands by the window, gazing out onto the street. At his
feet, a tin of black paint. In his hand, a fat paintbrush. ANGIE
is getting the bar ready. After a moment:

ANGIE. Hey, Frank. Helps if you dip the brush in the paint first.

FRANK. One of my brother's boys was supposed to come
    black out the windows. Who's manager here anyway?

ANGIE. Gee I was wondering that, cos I'm just a humble
    bartender working away and you're some man staring out
    the window watching them street kids.

FRANK. Why do I want to watch those wasters?

ANGIE. Maybe cos you got the hots for the blond boy.

FRANK *looks at her to shut her up. She shrugs. Pause.*

FRANK. I don't see no blond one.

ANGIE. How long do you give it?

FRANK. It?

ANGIE. This is the fourth bar we've opened in two years. It took them three weeks for the cops to shut the last place down. That's some kind of record.

FRANK. They want bigger payments. They're screwing us if you ask me. The Mayor's having one of his crackdowns, it'll blow over.

ANGIE. I don't know. They used to just raid. Now half the time they shut places down. Do you ever think there's got to be an easier way to make a living?

FRANK. Not with your qualifications.

ANGIE. I meant you. You got the connections.

FRANK. I made money on the last joint even in three weeks. I was thinking we could build a little stage over there. I'll get my brother's boys on to that too. And maybe start up some cards and roulette upstairs.

ANGIE. Do gays like to gamble?

FRANK. How should I know?

RUBY *enters.*

RUBY. Somebody fill me a glass then fill me in on the conversation so I can sparkle in it.

ANGIE. Ruby!

FRANK. We ain't open. Gimme a hand here.

ANGIE. Where've you been?

RUBY. Around. Had to find another bar to dazzle, didn't I. This is... nice.

ANGIE. I thought maybe they'd put you in jail after the raid.

RUBY. Honey, they kept me in two nights. Me, three queens and a drunk. Another drunk. They'd have kept me in longer but they didn't like the singing. What are you calling it?

FRANK. The Baker's Tavern. Joint used to be a bakery.

RUBY. Original.

FRANK. It sounds respectable. It sounds classy.

ANGIE. It justifies the prices.

FRANK *smiles and taps his forehead.*

FRANK. Didn't you read the sign?

RUBY. What sign?

FRANK. Aw, Jesus, they're supposed to have painted the name outside.

RUBY. You should open up in an old brothel next, Frank. The Whore's Inn. Maybe she is.

ANGIE. You gonna help me, Ruby?

RUBY. Setting up a new bar on dismal resources is my speciality. In Vietnam I created a whole movie theatre from a hut and couple of sheets from the meds. We had popcorn. Good morning, Frank.

FRANK. You stop talking. Angie, did I say for you to stop working? I'm the boss here, remember.

RUBY. Honey, you don't pay me, remember.

FRANK. I let you in for free though. (*Pause.*) What the hell do you do?

RUBY. Are you showing interest in another human being, Frank? (*Grandly.*) I have a glamorous job working in design and sales in a top-class clothing establishment.

FRANK. Does he?

ANGIE. Yeah, a glamorous part-time job in a second-hand clothes shop.

RUBY. It keeps me in underwear. Which really sets off my ankles, know what I'm saying, Franky boy. And today I must look my best. Josh is back.

ANGIE. You heard from him?

RUBY. I got a postcard.

He fishes a postcard out of somewhere and hands it to ANGIE. *It is a picture of Queen Elizabeth II.*

ANGIE (*reads it*). 'Dear Ruby. I thought you would like to see what a real queen looks like. Yours, Josh.' Romantic.

RUBY. He put a kiss. (*Points at the kiss.*) Why don't you like him?

ANGIE. I like him. He's just different. (*Beat.*) He's going places.

RUBY. Well, just now he's coming back from places. (*Beat.*) You think he's too special for me?

ANGIE. Ain't so special that it stopped you going home with a stevedore Thursday night.

RUBY. I hadn't had a stevedore before.

ANGIE. I think he likes you heaps. I just don't think that's enough for things to last, in the end.

RUBY. Honey. Things don't last. They just go on happening a day at a time. And another day, and another. Then you look in the mirror and, whoops, you got old. (*Beat.*) I shall wear pearls.

ANGIE (*laughs*). I just know I wouldn't be going home with a dock worker if I had someone that handsome and clever.

FRANK. They say opposites attract.

RUBY. That's true, I heard good things about your wife, Frank, so / maybe –

FRANK. You planning on doing any work?

RUBY. How *are* the lovely wife and daughter?

FRANK. Expensive. Daughter wants to go to college. Or the wife wants her to.

RUBY. I'm sure it's worth selling your soul for.

FRANK. Angie, if Officer Kirkpatrick comes in, give him this.

He hands her an envelope.

RUBY. Romantic, did you spray it? The sweet scent of corruption...

FRANK. Cut the naive shit, Ruby. It keeps the cops off our backs, it gives you and your faggot friends somewhere to drink.

RUBY. Let's see how much longer that lasts, Frank.

FRANK. Yeah yeah yeah.

RUBY. This little set-up's gonna end soon enough just like prohibition ended, you know? Ask your daddy about that.

FRANK. Ruby. Back room.

FRANK *exits to the back room.*

RUBY. Wish I had a dollar for every man you'd said that to.

ANGIE. If you did you'd spend it all here anyway. (*Beat.*) I only meant don't get hurt, Ruby. Or hurt him.

RUBY. Frank?

ANGIE. Josh.

RUBY. Cynic.

He exits after FRANK. ANGIE *puts a record on the record player: 'My Generation' by The Who.* ANGIE *starts off by tidying the bar but starts to get into the music, she starts to play an imaginary guitar and does some headbanging.*

DANNY *enters. He is in plain clothes.* ANGIE *doesn't see him.* DANNY *watches her a while. He grins, takes out a cigarette lighter and waves it.* ANGIE *turns around and sees him, she turns the music off.*

ANGIE. You always creep up on women like that?

DANNY. Just admiring the performance.

ANGIE *picks up the envelope and hands it to him.*

ANGIE. I'm assuming this is what you been sent for.

DANNY takes the envelope. Grins and holds out his hand.

DANNY. Danny Kirkpatrick.

She doesn't respond.

And you are?

ANGIE. Elizabeth Taylor.

DANNY. Yeah, course. Well, Liz, if... if Richard can spare you tonight, how about coming out for a meal with me.

ANGIE. I got a premiere.

DANNY. Huh?

ANGIE. I don't want to go out with you. Okay?

She turns and starts to tidy the bar.

DANNY. You know you're breaking the law here.

ANGIE turns back to face him.

ANGIE. I know that that's rich coming from you. (*Points at the envelope.*) Don't spend it all at once, Officer.

RUBY enters from the back room.

RUBY. It's the devil with the blue dress on. Get the hell out of my bar!

DANNY. Excuse me, sir, but you are not the manager of this bar. Mr Ravelli is.

RUBY. Get out of my bar!

RUBY charges at DANNY, punches him and gets him in a headlock. As DANNY struggles out of it, JOSH enters. He is wearing a nice suit, and has a suitcase and a couple of bags. He puts them down and rushes to RUBY, pulling him off DANNY.

JOSH. Ruby!

DANNY shows JOSH his ID.

Shit.

DANNY. Step away, sir, or you're under arrest. This... man just... ran at me.

JOSH. Ruby, you idiot.

RUBY. Listen to him, why dontcha. Hey, you came straight to see me?

DANNY (*to* RUBY). You, quiet. You're under arrest.

ANGIE (*slightly flirty*). Officer, can I have a little chat with you.

ANGIE *encourages* DANNY *to move away from* RUBY *and* JOSH.

He just got a bit excited. It ain't easy for him. He's still getting over 'Nam.

DANNY. He assaulted a police officer.

ANGIE. Oh! Are you hurt, honey?

DANNY. Oh, no, I'm –

ANGIE. Look, Officer, Danny, isn't it? About us going out tonight. How about a movie?

DANNY. You'll come out with me?

ANGIE. Sure. If you just forget about the last few minutes.

DANNY. Aw, I don't know.

ANGIE. Whatever movie you want.

DANNY. Yeah, okay. On one condition.

ANGIE. What's that?

DANNY. We go and see *Jungle Book*.

ANGIE. *Jungle Book*?

DANNY. I'm a sucker for Disney.

ANGIE. Me too. Well, drop by here Thursday at eight.

DANNY. Aw, but it's only Monday.

ANGIE. I got a bar to open before then.

DANNY. Okay. Sure. Thursday at eight.

ANGIE. See you then.

DANNY *exits*.

RUBY. I don't need you to fight my battles.

ANGIE. You assaulted him, Rube. If you think I'm visiting you in jail every week to update you on *Peyton Place*, think again.

JOSH. Me either.

RUBY. I can look after myself. You going to tell him about Benjy?

ANGIE. I don't hide Benjy from no one. And it's not a real date, remember?

RUBY. What if he falls for you?

ANGIE. He's handsome and he has a job, Ruby, he ain't gonna fall for me. Anyway I don't need your lectures. Josh. Welcome home.

JOSH. Thanks. When are you opening this place?

ANGIE. Tonight.

JOSH *looks around, unconvinced*.

You had a good vacation?

JOSH. Ha. It was a work trip, Angie. We're expanding into Europe so I was helping set up the London office. (*Beat.*) But yeah it was swell!

ANGIE. Great. Now be a lamb and go away, I got a bar to get ready. I wish Frank'd send me on a work trip.

ANGIE *exits to the back room*.

RUBY. How did you even know about this joint?

JOSH. I went to your place to see if you were there. Bumped into Stanley.

RUBY. Did she try it on?

JOSH. Not this time.

RUBY. I wanna be naked and high with you.

RUBY *kisses* JOSH.

JOSH. Yeah... I'm kinda tired, Ruby. I should go home.

RUBY. I'll come. (*Pause.*) What?

JOSH. Nothing, it's just that my place will be clean, and there's a proper bed, and... I don't want to see you right now.

RUBY. You just got back.

JOSH. Yeah I know and I walk in here and what the hell was that about? With the cop? We talked about this, honey, you got to –

RUBY. I ain't got to do anything. I'm fed up with it. We got Mafia on the one side and cops on the other and sometimes you just wanna shout, fuck the fuck away from me, I'm trying to dance here.

JOSH. It's the middle of the afternoon.

RUBY. Don't be smart. If people like you had the balls.

JOSH. People like what?

RUBY. People with decent jobs and rich moms and dads and –

JOSH. Mom and Dad work hard. I got one life. I'm not going to waste it fighting. I already have you, don't I? (*Beat.*) That guy could have arrested me just now.

RUBY. Well, there you go. (*Pause.*) In Vietnam –

JOSH. Here we go.

RUBY (*warmly*). Fuck you. We had to do some stupid dangerous shit. Some general would decide we suddenly gotta move our entire camp five hundred yards overnight, or he'd have us befriending some stupid village to 'improve their lives' or some crap, and we'd end up giving them our every last Band-Aid and cigarette and they'd still tell the VC our every move. We'd get sent out at stupid o'clock to get shot at in the dark and if you were lucky you made it back without a massive leech stuck to your dick but at least, and this is my point, at least when some fucker died he got sent home a hero. A hero with a leech on his dick. We're scum. You want a beer?

JOSH. No.

RUBY. If the coloureds can fight for their rights, then so can we.

JOSH. Hitting one bent cop is not a march, Ruby.

RUBY. But if we all got together –

JOSH. If it's important to you, why don't you get involved with those campaigners. The Mattachine group, is it? They're organised.

RUBY. If I want a discussion group, I'll go to church, at least they do songs. The fuck they ever achieved?

JOSH. Just check them out, okay? You're good with words. You could write their little pamphlets and stuff.

RUBY. Don't patronise me.

JOSH. Sorry. I didn't mean to.

RUBY. Maybe you're right, Maybe this can be my thing. I need a 'thing'. As queen of the flame queens I shall offer leadership and action.

FRANK *enters from the back room.*

FRANK (*to* JOSH). Hey, sunshine. Stop yapping. You'd get that window painted sooner if you had a, a paintbrush in your hand.

JOSH. Excuse me?

RUBY. Josh, Frank. Frank. This is Josh. One of your previous establishment's loyal customers.

FRANK. Thought you were one of my brother's boys. Get out, we're closed.

FRANK *goes to the bar, reaches for a telephone behind it.*

JOSH. Okay…

FRANK (*amused at himself*). You been at a funeral or something?

RUBY. He's been to London.

FRANK. Am I supposed to be impressed?

> FRANK *tries the phone. It's not working. He bashes it a bit.*

Shit. (*To* JOSH.) Come on, get out of here.

> FRANK *exits into the back.*

JOSH. Can I give you your presents? I want to see if you love them.

RUBY. Come back to the palace.

JOSH (*smiles*). Yes, your majesty.

> *They kiss.*

RUBY (*gently, oddly*). I want you to hurt me.

> JOSH *looks at him.*

JOSH. Take me home.

> RUBY *picks* JOSH's *suitcase up for him and carries it out. They exit.*

Scene Two

The Baker's Inn at night. There is now an ageing jukebox installed. A record player is on or behind the bar. ANGIE *is writing names onto labels and sticking them onto bottles of alcohol.* RUBY *enters.*

ANGIE. You're here early. It's still light outside.

RUBY. The day you start serving breakfast pancakes is the day I never leave this joint.

ANGIE. Your aspiration brings tears to my eyes, Rube.

RUBY (*half to himself*). Or do they make raids on unlicensed pancake houses. Probably.

RUBY *goes to the jukebox and browses.*

No, no they do. You know that? Twice I been in that juice bar. Twelfth of Always.

ANGIE. Tenth.

RUBY. Place where they let the queer kids dance. Although they still don't let them sit too close together to eat their ice cream – what's that about, is it about spillage, do you think? Two times when I've been there they flicked on this huge chandelier they got, real bright, and all the kids stopped dancing. Turns out it's a sign means the cops are there, I mean this is a fucking juice bar. I had a lady cop call me 'madam' and ask if she should search me or get her male colleague to do it. I said, hell, lady, why don't you both have a squeeze but wash your fucking hands first, both of you. I wasn't even in drag. Just a bit of make-up and my shirt tied up.

Puts a track on. 'Forget Me Not' by Martha and the Vandellas starts playing.

Mafia running ice-cream parlours. It's not manly. Later, alligator. (*Goes to exit.*)

ANGIE. Why do you always do that?

RUBY. What?

ANGIE. Put a song on then walk out.

RUBY. Benevolence.

RUBY *exits.* ANGIE *carries on.* JIMMY *enters. He's in his teens. Eyeliner. Skinny.*

JIMMY. I'll get a whiskey please.

ANGIE. Who let you in?

JIMMY. Who let you out of the zoo?

ANGIE. Yeah, okay, out.

JIMMY. The bitch on the door let me in.

ANGIE. The bitch?

JIMMY (*slowly*). The man on the door.

ANGIE. Charlie. (*Looks at* JIMMY.) Figures.

JIMMY. I don't know. Fat old bitch… He's probably why it's so quiet in here.

ANGIE. It's early. And we only opened two nights ago.

JIMMY. They should have someone like me work here.

ANGIE. Someone like you, huh? Here's the thing: they don't much like queers to work here. They like you at arm's length.

JIMMY. Guy on the door's queer. He was looking at me like his tongue was already inside me.

ANGIE. He don't brush his teeth too often.

JIMMY. I don't wipe my ass too often.

ANGIE (*laughs*). They put a gay guy on the door cos it's the man on the door who gets it in the neck when Lilly Law comes. How old are you?

JIMMY. I love this song. Did you know it's about waiting for a soldier to come home? I always play it at the Tenth. (*Starts singing along for a moment.*) I'm gonna marry a soldier. When I was thirteen I had a boyfriend who was a cop. Lived in his apartment. Nice place. I'd make him breakfast and we'd have it out on the balcony. I'm good at that kinda stuff. Then I'd go back to bed and he'd go to work. It was nice in the summer, you could sit out there and smoke dope.

ANGIE. You got any advice for a date with a cop?

JIMMY. Any advice on where to get a fucking drink?

ANGIE *picks up a bottle and a glass.*

Two. My friend's coming.

ANGIE. Your friend.

She pours two drinks. Looks at the label on the bottle.

Hey, whaddya know, you get to be Martin Luther King tonight.

JIMMY. Who?

ANGIE. He's the name on the bottle. We're a bottle club. We're not licensed to sell alcohol so people bring their own and leave it here with their name on it. That's eighty cents.

JIMMY. You just said –

ANGIE. It's a scam, who knew.

JIMMY *gets out a wedge of notes.*

Where'd you get that?

JIMMY. Place where I could get money and a bath. (*Grins.*) Smell me?

ANGIE. Thank you. No.

JIMMY. Eighty cents, that normal?

ANGIE. This joint ain't normal. You a street kid?

JIMMY. Village girl. Jimmy. Miss Jimmy. Where's the dancing? I wanna dance.

ANGIE. In the back room but I told you it's early. We don't get dancing out front till late. You were gonna give me advice on dating a cop.

JIMMY. I dunno. Be pretty. Listen to his boring stories. Let him beat you about a bit. Steal his money.

ANGIE. Can't wait. (*Beat.*) Hot night, huh. Where's your friend.

JIMMY. I dunno. Yeah it's hot.

He takes off his shirt, ties it round his waist, he has a vest on underneath. Sniffs himself.

Clean. (*Beat.*) Only took it today.

ANGIE. What did you do to your shoulder?

JIMMY. I didn't do nothing to my shoulder, what did you do to your face? (*Beat.*) I didn't do nothing to my shoulder. Just hurt it climbing out a window. Worth it though, came out with a loaded wallet.

RUBY *enters from the street.*

ANGIE. Back so soon, Rube, it's like we got you on elastic.

RUBY. Went to get these.

He has some pamphlets, and slaps them on the bar.

ANGIE. You said you want to marry a soldier. Now's your chance.

JIMMY. I said I'm *gonna* marry a soldier.

RUBY. Oooooh, look, we got us a little boy! I'm so happy. What shall we call her?

JIMMY. He ain't a soldier.

RUBY. Didn't your mamma ever tell you not to judge a book by its cover?

JIMMY. Didn't your mamma take your balls out of her dirty mouth long enough to give you some fucking manners? You a soldier?

ANGIE. Year in Vietnam.

JIMMY. You?!

RUBY. Ten months. It was meant to be a year. Sit on my knee and I'll tell you all about it. No don't. Stand. I don't want my clothes dirty.

JIMMY. You want that you can meet me down the piers with cash and queue for it like anyone else.

RUBY. Little girl, if I want street garbage I can go down the trucks and pick up a sack full for free.

ANGIE. What's the trucks?

RUBY. Trucks… rhymes with fucks… No seriously, you don't wanna know.

ANGIE. You can no longer shock me.

RUBY. I'm sparing you, honey.

JIMMY. The trucks is the trucks down by the river where they load them up from the boats. They leave them empty at night and guys fuck in them cos it's dark and secluded.

ANGIE. You dirty boys.

RUBY. You go to the trucks?

JIMMY. Used to. One time I got beat up though and nearly got
drowned in the river and another time a cop put me in jail for
the night and another time I had money and someone stole it
so I don't now not even with the other girls. I'm gonna
dance.

*He shimmies a little across the room but stops, unties his
shirt from his waist, and pulls it back on, self-conscious.*

ANGIE. Honey, it's okay. You won't be the first boy with scars
on his body to get asked to dance in this place.

JIMMY. No one usually asks about 'em. That's all.

As JIMMY *exits to the back room,* FRANK *comes out of the
room. There is a moment's vague recognition, which* JIMMY
pretends hasn't happened. FRANK *says nothing.*

RUBY *goes to the jukebox.*

FRANK (*looks about the place grandly*). You'd never believe
we made this place on pocket money, would you?

ANGIE. You probably would, Frank. It's the leftover black
paint from the last place and a few posters.

RUBY. Yeah, what is it, you miss your jail cell or something?

ANGIE. You know that kid?

FRANK. No. Why?

ANGIE. Smart kid.

FRANK. That right? (*Beat.*) Well, you're looking at one smart
kid right here, kid.

RUBY (*to the jukebox*). I am begging you. I am on my knees,
begging you, sweet shiny shiny magic music box, play the
fucking song.

He looks at ANGIE *over his shoulder.*

(*Conspiratorial whisper.*) She don't know I'm not really on
my knees. She's just a jukebox.

ANGIE. First time for everything.

FRANK. We'll hit profit no time. Genovese's gonna be very impressed with me.

ANGIE. Who?

FRANK. An investor.

RUBY. I love how you make it sound like a legitimate business. What, so someone actually puts money into this?

FRANK. He makes things happen. He's gonna see my potential with this place.

ANGIE. You think? (*Beat.*) Are you meant to tell me this stuff?

FRANK. You? I can tell you anything, Angie.

RUBY *has backed away across the room and charges full steam at the jukebox, which he hurls himself at with a crash. A song plays: 'Trains and Boats and Planes' by Dionne Warwick.*

Hey hey hey! It's new.

RUBY. No it's not.

ANGIE. Sad song. You're in a strange way tonight.

RUBY. I am.

ANGIE. Wanna talk?

RUBY. No. (*Beat.*) Where's Josh? That boy works far too long. Ain't good for a body spending so long in a stuffy old office.

ANGIE. It ain't so good for a body spending so much time in this stuffy joint.

RUBY. I'm your best customer.

ANGIE. Was talking about me.

FRANK. That envelope get picked up?

ANGIE. Uh-huh.

FRANK *takes a leaflet from the bar.*

FRANK. What's this? (*To* ANGIE.) Get these out of here.

RUBY. It's a gay bar.

FRANK. You take this political shit out of here, now, you want cops seeing it?

RUBY. Yes of course I fucking do, why do you think I wrote it, you piece of shit.

JIMMY *enters as* FRANK *picks up a handful of the leaflets. He rips them angrily, throws the pieces in* RUBY*'s face and squares up to him for a moment. Then:*

FRANK. Angie, clean this up. (*Beat.*) If I wanted to argue with a moron with stupid hair I'd stay at home more often.

RUBY. Cocksucker.

JOSH *enters.*

JOSH. Hi, Angie. Hey, lover.

JIMMY. Hi. I'm Miss Jimmy.

JOSH. Josh.

RUBY *pushes* JIMMY *out of the way.*

RUBY. Come back when your balls drop, junior.

JIMMY. Perhaps he wants the nice fresh meat, old man. Not the tough mouldy old stuff.

JOSH *laughs and kisses* RUBY. JIMMY *wanders off.*

FRANK. I got work to do. (*To* JIMMY.) See you, kid.

FRANK *exits.* ANGIE *picks up a leaflet.*

ANGIE. Aw, Jesus, Rube, when did you get involved in this gay rights stuff?

RUBY. Since I checked out the Mattachine geeks. I wrote that shit myself.

JOSH. Fast work.

ANGIE. You can't leave them here. Frank'll blow a piston.

RUBY. How's the high-flying world of finance?

JOSH (*kissing* RUBY). It is swell.

ANGIE. Guess that's banker for good.

JOSH. Leveridge called me in to his office today.

RUBY. Anyone else's eyelids drooping already?

JOSH. To thank me for securing the Morganti deal. And guess what –

RUBY. He slipped out his dentures and gave you the best oral sex you have ever had right there on the twenty-fourth floor.

JOSH. Second best, baby.

ANGIE. Please.

JOSH. I'm getting my own office, and my own secretary.

RUBY. Oh, sir! Get the gold-plated typewriter ready.

JOSH. You know I can't employ you.

RUBY. Thank you, I know. I was joking, don't panic. Pity though. I'd be top of the pool. (*Brandishes a pamphlet.*) Turns out I can type.

JIMMY *saunters over.*

JIMMY (*to* JOSH). I like your suit. I'd look good in a suit. (*Pats it.*) Nice chest!

JOSH (*laughs*). Thanks!

JIMMY. You bored with the old Vietnam nurse yet?

RUBY. I told you, beat it, junior. And no comments on 'Nam, if you ain't been you got no right to comment.

JIMMY. I ain't been to the Moon but I know it's as big, pale and lonely as your ass.

RUBY. Shut your fucking mouth. Unless you spent ten months ducking bullets trying to defend a country from maniacs. Took out more of the little shits than anyone in the unit and I come back here and find out the world hates me for it.

JOSH. I don't hate you.

JIMMY. You can't be queer in the military.

RUBY. Are you kidding me? I had so much cock coming at me I was thinking, if only there was a way to save some of this cock for another time. But you know, I hear it goes off. (*Pause*.) Even had a boyfriend out there.

JIMMY (*to* ANGIE). Two more whiskies please.

RUBY. Fucking ignorant.

ANGIE. Your friend turned up?

JIMMY. No... Kinda weird, it's his birthday.

ANGIE. But you want two whiskies?

JIMMY. A guy in the back asked me to dance.

ANGIE *pours him the drinks*.

Thanks.

ANGIE. A pleasure, Miss Jimmy.

JIMMY. What's your name?

ANGIE. Audrey Hepburn.

JIMMY *heads to the back room.* FRANK *enters and they pass each other...*

FRANK. Hey.

JIMMY. Hey.

FRANK. It is you.

JIMMY. Usually is.

FRANK (*quiet*). You don't remember?

JIMMY. I don't remember.

FRANK *grabs* JIMMY *by his collar*.

FRANK. You stole my wallet. And I'd already given you money.

JIMMY. I ain't got your wallet.

Pause. FRANK *lets go*.

FRANK. Okay. (*Beat*.) Do you like my bar? Did you dance?

JIMMY. A man asked me to dance. I never got asked to dance before. You work here?

FRANK. Kid, do I look like a waiter?

JIMMY. Yeah. A little.

FRANK. I knew you'd taken my wallet. But I'm not a mean man. I can afford to lose a few notes. See, I'm a businessman. I'd like to give you the chance to make amends. We could maybe chat about that upstairs, how we can help each other out.

JIMMY. Okay.

FRANK. Stop by tomorrow night.

JIMMY. Sure.

> FRANK *exits to the street.* JIMMY *comes back over.*

That guy own this joint?

ANGIE. Don't get mixed up with him. You need to rent your ass, go some place else.

JIMMY. Where?

ANGIE (*laughs*). Just not him.

JIMMY. He's gonna give me work.

ANGIE. He has a weakness for pretty boys.

JIMMY (*to* JOSH). What about you, Josh? Do you have a weakness for pretty boys?

> JOSH *smiles.*

ANGIE. It's not Frank that gets hurt.

JIMMY. I don't get hurt. It's just how things are.

RUBY. And that, ladies and gentlemen, is the fucking motto of the queens of New York. That's why we're still hiding out in shitty bars. No offence, Angie.

JIMMY. I kinda like it here.

JOSH. So does he. You like working here, Angie?

ANGIE. Uh. Sure.

RUBY gives JIMMY a pamphlet.

RUBY. You should get involved. Protest.

JIMMY. Do you pay?

RUBY. It ain't about money. It's about our rights.

JIMMY. I left a guy waiting.

He shoves the pamphlet in his pocket, picks up the drinks and exits out back. As he does:

RUBY. Hey, kid. You left your price tag on. (*Pause.*) Could lick him for a week.

JOSH (*laughs*). Yeah, look at you, recruiting him! Hands off.

He takes one of RUBY's pamphlets.

You didn't put your name on it.

RUBY. They wouldn't let me. One day I'll have my name on the front of the *Village Voice*. No, *The New York Times*.

JOSH. When you get arrested, yeah.

RUBY. I wouldn't mind that. Would be worth it. (*Beat.*) It's gonna kick off soon, you know? People are getting more angry when there's a raid. It's gonna kick off and we're gonna be there.

JOSH. Come on, relax, climb down from the mountain a while. Let's have fun, I had a long day.

RUBY. Sorry. Tomorrow. I'll be in a good mood tomorrow. I think I'm gonna sing tomorrow.

ANGIE. Your debut in the new place and I'll miss it, hon. I got my date with destiny. Well, Danny.

RUBY tuts.

JOSH. C'mon, you wanna dance?

RUBY. Always, baby. Lead the way.

Scene Three

ANGIE*'s apartment. Late evening. The room is a bedroom-cum-living area.* ANGIE *and* DANNY *arrive. They have a bag of beers, and they each have one open.* DANNY *dances around the room like a monkey.* ANGIE *laughs.*

DANNY *sings a few lines from the chorus of 'I Wanna Be Like You' from* The Jungle Book.

ANGIE. Sit down, you'll wake Benjy. Jeez, what would you be like if we'd actually seen it?

DANNY. I've seen it already. Three times. Shoulda known it wouldn't still be showing. Sorry.

ANGIE. Was you that wanted to see it, idiot. I liked *Goodbye, Columbus*. I like a romance. It was like you and me but the wrong way round.

DANNY. How do you mean?

ANGIE. I ain't the good little family girl in the room. (*Pause.*) Sit down?

He does. A moment.

DANNY. Your babysitter was angry.

ANGIE. I'm late back. She's tired.

DANNY. You know, I'm a cop, I can handle queers and organised crime but, man, a coloured girl in a rage sure gives me the frights.

ANGIE. She's cool.

DANNY. So. How long have you had... Benjy?

ANGIE. Since he was born.

DANNY. I meant that.

ANGIE. He's not a dog. Benjy is nearly three and – and I know you won't believe this – he is even cuter than his mom. Mainly because he gets a decent night's sleep once in a while. And yeah he is the only man in my life.

DANNY. Wow.

ANGIE. Is that 'wow that's great' or 'wow I need to get the fuck out of here'? I know what you're thinking.

DANNY. No, no I –

ANGIE. Yeah, 'wow, I struck gold with this chick'. You want another beer?

DANNY. Let me.

ANGIE. I got 'em.

She opens two more.

DANNY. We should take it slow.

ANGIE. I'm sorry, Officer, am I sitting improperly close?

DANNY. I meant the beer. You won't be used to drinks that ain't watered down.

ANGIE. Nothing gets past you gumballs, huh.

DANNY. Gumballs?

ANGIE. The thing on the roof of your cars – the light – it looks like a bubblegum machine.

DANNY. I guess.

ANGIE. Yeah I don't see it either.

DANNY. I never made out in a room next to kid before.

ANGIE. Don't let me break your home run. You're here for a beer.

DANNY. Okay. (*Beat.*) Cool. (*Pause.*) So where's his dad?

ANGIE. 'Nam. I told you I ain't with nobody. Soon as he heard I was knocked up he couldn't get a uniform on fast enough. Mary's great though.

DANNY. The coloured girl? The babysitter?

ANGIE. Yes, she's Benjy's aunt. She looks after him most of the time these days.

DANNY. Huh – but she's...

ANGIE. Nothing gets past you, huh, Mr Mannix. I left my kid
with a black chick? Arrest me, Officer. Yeah, she's black.
He's kinda black.

DANNY. That's cool.

ANGIE. Right.

DANNY. I ain't a dinosaur. My little sister's teaching me to be
more liberal.

ANGIE. You wanna watch that in your line of work. (*Beat.*) So
I'm just what your mother dreamed of, right? Older woman,
single mom, mixed kid.

She cups his face, studies him.

Let me see. Daddy's a cop too.

DANNY. I told you that.

ANGIE. Senior. Takes you and your brother to the game some
days with his cop buddies.

DANNY. My brother's in Vietnam.

ANGIE. Yeah, with Benjy's dad cleaning his boots for him.
What is it with that place, we're really missing the party,
aren't we? (*Beat.*) Sundays you meet up. Go to church then
back to the family home. Mom cooks a turkey. She doesn't
say it because she's not that kind of woman but she's
thinking, 'Why's my handsome boy alone? He needs a nice
older girl that hangs out with queers and doesn't see her
family and has a little black kid.'

DANNY. That's mothers.

ANGIE. Tell me about it.

DANNY. It doesn't matter what Mom thinks.

He kisses her.

ANGIE. You taste of beer and popcorn.

DANNY. You should come be a detective.

ANGIE. Switch sides? We'd lose this exquisite tension.

They kiss again.

I'm just gonna look in on him. Grab yourself a beer.

ANGIE *exits*, DANNY *gets a beer and sits down, starts to sing, quieter than before.*

DANNY (*singing*). Og oobie doo.

ANGIE *enters.*

ANGIE. Snug as a bug.

DANNY (*singing*). I wanna be like you.

ANGIE. Like hell you do. Hey, shush now.

DANNY. Yeah, you don't want the neighbours callin' the cops.

ANGIE. They won't. They're gay. You wanna be like me, I can get you a stint on the bar. I'd always dreamed of working on the hat counter at Macy's.

DANNY. Hats?

ANGIE. Yeah, you know. Hats. It's funny cos my mom's a hairdresser but I like hats. Hats with flowers, hats with ribbons, hats with bows, hats with –

DANNY. You wanna shut up about hats?

DANNY *grabs her, they kiss, this time for longer.*

Still wanna talk about hats?

ANGIE. Yeah.

He kisses her again.

DANNY. Doesn't it bother you you got queers living next door and you got a kid?

ANGIE. It bothers me I got the mob on the doorstep and the cops in their pockets and I got a kid. (*Beat.*) Why don't you just shut all the illegal bars down?

DANNY. You'd be out of a job.

ANGIE. Spare me your concern. Hey and listen, mister, if you think –

DANNY. Yeah yeah if I think I'm gonna stay I can think again, you don't do it on first dates. It's cool.

ANGIE. Oh. No, I wasn't gonna say – but yeah. Yes. (*Beat*.) Though I guess you could, you could argue, you could make the case that, that the movie was our first date and then this is our second. (*Beat*.) I mean, if you were gonna not be a gentleman. That's what I'd probably do.

She undoes a button on his shirt.

DANNY. Hello, Columbus.

She pulls off DANNY's shirt.

The scene dims, fades into the next.

Scene Four

The Baker's Tavern, the same night. The bar is busy, dark and smokey. JOSH is there. A sense of others. RUBY gives JOSH a kiss then steps onto the makeshift stage. The music stops and RUBY addresses the crowd. They laugh and react.

RUBY. Now, ladies and… well, it's a hot night so let's be generous and say 'gentlemen'… ladies and gentlemen, you know how it is. It was the middle of the afternoon here in our sedate little village. I'd been out of bed at least a half-hour. Taking a stroll in the sunshine with what might have been a stone in my shoe but which I like to think was a spring in my step.

And there he is. Twenty yards in front, walking down the street with a perfect little tush bouncing in faded denim. Narrow waist you'd wanna wrap just about any part of you around. Shoulders so broad they're stretching his shirt like sailcloth. And yes, dirty blond curls like the golden hair of a fallen angel.

He knows I'm looking. Sure as hell. A glance over one of those shoulders and he slows it right down. He stops. Why, he seems to have grown interested in something in that window. Only here's the thing, it's that shitty drugstore on the corner that's been empty six months. Well, as you can imagine, this has aroused my already growing... curiosity. I stop and I stand beside him.

Now, my mother brought me up to be a friendly girl to strangers, ladies and gentlemen, if only for the extra income. So I glance across at my mystery man. And he turns his face toward me to meet my gaze... and fuck me, ladies and gentlemen, pardon my Spanish, but fuck me what an ugly fucking face. I actually flinch. Seriously, I'm wondering how the hell he managed to stare into that shop window so long without the glass shattering. Putting a face like that on a body like that. It's like your mamma baked your favourite apple pie then squeezed a crap out right on top of it.

Man, he's so ugly he's probably an undercover cop or something. I got trapped like that once before. Well now. Once I've managed to swallow back down the bile in my mouth, I am polite but firm. Not that kinda firm, that thing was soft as the first golden hairs in a fifteen-year-old's butt crack.

I said to him the only thing I could say. I told him, honey, you see me again, you see me walkin' down the street, you just walk on by...

A record plays, 'Walk On By' by Dionne Warwick. RUBY *begins to sing along. He makes a bit of a fuss of* JOSH *as he sings.*

A few lines, and then we fade into the next scene.

Scene Five

ANGIE*'s apartment. Early the next morning, the start of a hot, sunny day.* DANNY *and* ANGIE*'s clothes are on the floor.* DANNY *stands at the open window in his underpants. City sounds.*

ANGIE *enters, wearing* DANNY*'s shirt.*

ANGIE. I'll be back in a minute, honey. You just wait like a good boy.

DANNY. I'm going nowhere.

ANGIE. Not you, him. Don't you have to work?

DANNY. Not yet.

ANGIE. You from here, right?

DANNY. Upstate. You?

ANGIE. Across the river.

DANNY. My dad always said, this city's got everything that's right and everything that's wrong in it. And every day you gotta choose what kinda man you are.

ANGIE. Are we in church now?

DANNY. Know what I love? That you can point at a window out there and wonder who lives in that apartment. Maybe someone famous. Maybe someone really rich. Someone foreign.

ANGIE. Someone crying.

DANNY. Plenty of those.

ANGIE. You must get to see inside some pretty nice homes in your job.

DANNY. Some. See those kids down there? They're stupid. Half of them have got homes to go to. They live like wild dogs and every few weeks we find one beaten half to death cos he robbed the wrong guy. We pulled one out of the river three weeks back. An elderly couple spotted his arm. They said there was a girl in the river. He had nail polish on one hand and the long hair and that was all they saw.

ANGIE. You don't know what his home was like. (*Beat.*) Hell, who am I to talk?

DANNY. I'm sure you do a great job.

ANGIE. It's parents like that you should be locking up.

DANNY. It's the kids' choice. What do they know at that age? (*Beat.*) I wouldn't normally say this but you're a woman of the world.

ANGIE. Thank you...

DANNY. When guys are young they have thoughts and they get confused about other boys. It doesn't mean anything. Not enough to wreck your life over.

ANGIE. Maybe it shouldn't wreck their lives.

DANNY. You make your choices.

ANGIE. Did you get confused?

DANNY. I didn't say that! Come on, they're men. They'll sleep with anything, it's how men are.

ANGIE. And now I feel special.

DANNY. No no no what I'm getting at is... Well, so big deal they like to sleep with men more than they like to sleep with women. Why ruin your life over it? Get married. Get a job. Have kids and a nice house. Close your eyes and think about... whatever if it gets you by. Find a buddy. Pay someone. But no, they gotta make it their whole life at the expense of anything else. So they create their own dirty little world. And then they get screwed over. It's stupid.

ANGIE. Ruby fought in Vietnam. Josh is on Wall Street. That's real world. They're normal people.

DANNY. Ruby's nuts.

ANGIE. Okay, not Ruby. He attacked a jukebox last night. Sometimes he carries a chain round with him, like a weapon. He's really nuts. That's why they kicked him out of the military. Not because he was queer. (*Pause.*) What's the story on Frank?

DANNY. What do you mean?

ANGIE. His older brother's got the contracts for half the city's garbage removal and Frank runs a little queer bar.

DANNY. You know the joke about the Ravelli boys. They both keep trash off the streets.

ANGIE *doesn't respond.*

You know him better than I do. Maybe it's his choice.

ANGIE. Maybe. (*Beat.*) I know he was in jail.

ANGIE *gets close to* DANNY. *Strokes his body.*

You know you want to tell me about your bad-boy world.

DANNY *laughs.*

You're ticklish!

DANNY. Yes, I am.

ANGIE *tickles him.*

Stop it!

She does.

ANGIE. Do you think Frank ever killed anyone?

DANNY *doesn't answer.*

Did he kill someone?

DANNY *doesn't answer.*

Okay...

Pause.

DANNY. That wasn't why he was in jail.

ANGIE. I know.

DANNY. We couldn't pin it on him.

ANGIE. What happens to the money we give you?

DANNY. Aw, hey, come on.

ANGIE. I'm curious, who gets it. You? The chief?

DANNY *starts to pull on his clothes.*

DANNY. It goes to a few people. A small amount goes to taking nosy but very pretty women to see a movie.

ANGIE. Well, you ain't getting no more return on that little investment.

DANNY. Aw, come on. Next time you got the babysitter.

ANGIE. Is when I'll be at work.

DANNY. Okay... Sorry... I kinda thought we had a nice time.

ANGIE. Yeah. We had a nice time.

DANNY. You don't like me?

ANGIE. I'm just trying to picture us five dates down the line.

DANNY. Yeah...

ANGIE. What happens next time you raid the bar? You gonna kiss me hello on the way in? (*Pause.*) You gonna bring me roses?

DANNY. I'll bring you a hat covered in roses. From Macy's.

ANGIE. You do that.

DANNY. You don't have to work there.

BENJY (*offstage*). Mom.

DANNY. I'll call you.

ANGIE. Bye.

DANNY *kisses her cheek and leaves.*

Okay, sweetie, let's get you dressed.

She exits.

Scene Six

RUBY*'s apartment. There is a mattress on the floor that serves as a bed. The room has its own little kitchen unit. There is a door out to a hallway and a bathroom. The place is untidy, the kitchen unit not very clean.*

It is morning. Bright, clean sunshine from the curtainless window. JOSH *and* RUBY *are asleep on the mattress, under a sheet.*

JOSH *wakes with a start.* RUBY *wakes.*

RUBY. You okay, baby?

JOSH. Bad dream. Sorry.

RUBY. Come here.

JOSH. Wait wait. (*Beat.*) Just give me a second.

RUBY. Thought I was the one that gets nightmares.

A moment.

JOSH. It was... you were... you'd killed someone.

RUBY. In Vietnam?

JOSH. No I was – it was like in the showers at the gym... you weren't in the dream but you'd murdered someone and I was, I was having to get rid of the...

RUBY. The body?

JOSH. Flesh, bits of... flesh. Pink. Pushing it down the drain holes... It was just... sad, I felt sad. (*Beat.*) Sorry. Hold me.

RUBY *laughs gently.*

What?

RUBY. I feel guilty now.

JOSH *laughs. Shuffles into* RUBY*'s embrace.*

JOSH. This is nice.

RUBY. Mmmmm.

RUBY *snuggles into* JOSH, *presses against him.*

JOSH. Hello…

RUBY. Hello.

Pause.

JOSH. Sorry I couldn't – last night.

RUBY. Sshhh. (*Kisses* JOSH*'s neck.*) I love fucking you.

RUBY *kisses him.*

It's fine. It's good.

JOSH. What's the time?

RUBY. Seven. Just gone.

JOSH. I need to get up.

RUBY. Stay.

JOSH. I have to go to work.

RUBY. I know.

JOSH *starts to get up.* RUBY *holds on to him.*

JOSH. Hey.

RUBY. No, listen, I been thinking.

JOSH. What about?

RUBY. I been thinking I think you have to stay here.

JOSH *laughs.* RUBY *kisses him.*

JOSH. Don't, my breath –

RUBY *kisses him again.*

RUBY. Morning.

JOSH. Morning. (*Beat.*) Hey, c'mon, let me go.

RUBY. Okay.

JOSH. Well go on then.

RUBY. No.

JOSH *starts laughing.*

JOSH. Ruby!

    RUBY *holds him*.

    (*Serious now*.) Get off.

RUBY (*awkward*). Okay. (*Beat*.) Sorry.

    JOSH *gets out of bed*.

    You want me to fix you some coffee?

JOSH (*surprised*). You gonna make me coffee? Sweetheart.

    RUBY *stays in bed a while*. JOSH *goes to the window*.

    How do you live in this shit-heap?

RUBY. The Village?

JOSH. You know what I mean.

RUBY. I don't live here. I sleep here.

JOSH. You got a towel?

RUBY. Over there.

    RUBY *points*. JOSH *looks where* RUBY *is pointing. He doesn't see a towel*.

    In the laundry.

    RUBY *gets out of bed, pulls a crumpled old towel from a pile of dirty clothes. Gives it to* JOSH. JOSH *sniffs it*.

JOSH. There's a lady in the street.

RUBY. A lady in the street?

JOSH. A woman just fell over in the street.

    They look.

RUBY. Shit. She dead?

JOSH. I think she's drunk.

    They look. RUBY *laughs*.

RUBY. That ain't a lady, it's Stanley. (*Pause*.) Coffee.

JOSH *stays at the window while* RUBY *looks in cupboards.*

If you don't like it here we could stay at your apartment. (*Pause.*) I'll cook.

JOSH. You can cook?

RUBY. I used to cook with my mom. (*Beat.*) I won't talk to your neighbours.

JOSH. You're just not exactly discreet.

RUBY. It was only the old lady on your landing. She liked me. I helped her move that massive crazy plant.

JOSH. You teased her.

RUBY. I told her I liked her dress.

JOSH. You hated her dress.

RUBY. So what. Made her smile.

JOSH. You told her you had one just like it but in blue.

RUBY *laughs.* JOSH *laughs.*

RUBY. I got in my head she was kinda lonely maybe.

JOSH. She's married. (*Beat.*) So I... I wanted to ask you something.

RUBY. Shit.

JOSH. What?

RUBY. Out of coffee. Sorry. I was gonna get some in.

JOSH. It's cool.

RUBY. Sorry.

RUBY *comes and holds* JOSH *from behind.*

You wanted to ask me something.

JOSH. Oh. Yes. Yeah... One of our clients is hosting a fundraising dinner for his charity. Handicapped kids I think. My boss hinted I should take a date.

RUBY. A date date?

JOSH. You know, just a date. It'll be fun. Well, it'll be boring
fun. Do you think you could ask Angie if she'd wanna come
with me?

RUBY. Angie?

JOSH. There'll be a band, and dancing. The wine will be great,
the food will be okay. I'd buy her a dress.

RUBY. Angie?

JOSH. You think she'd like it?

RUBY. No I think she'd hate it. Why Angie?

JOSH. See there's this girl at work. And I think she likes me.
No, she does like me, it's obvious and people joke about it.
She's always got something prepared to say to me, you
know? We get on well and we like the same books and the
same music and she's very pretty. Leveridge said if I didn't
have anyone to take, why didn't I take her? But if I go with
her we'd have a great time, and then I'd escort her home, and
then there we'd be, in a cab or standing on her doorstep in
the moonlight. And she'd want me to kiss her. At least she
might. Either way we'd have this great night and then she'd
want to see me again. And I wouldn't, so it seems cruel to
invite her in the first place. I thought if Angie –

RUBY. I think you should ask her yourself.

JOSH. Ruby, you didn't think…?

RUBY. No. Yeah. I dunno. Take the girl from work. (*Pause.*)
What are you doing tonight? You wanna see a movie?

JOSH *mimes a tennis swing.*

Who you playing ping-pong with?

JOSH. I'm playing tennis with Adam.

RUBY. Is he the hot one?

JOSH. He's married! I went to his wedding, remember.

RUBY. You need a ball girl?

JOSH. Ruby, did you sleep with anyone when I was away?

RUBY. What?

JOSH. But did you?

RUBY. You said it was cool if I wanted to.

JOSH. If you wanted to.

RUBY. You were away.

JOSH. For two weeks.

RUBY. Three weeks.

JOSH. Nearly three weeks.

RUBY. Yeah. I slept with someone. (*Pause*.) Two people. But it was lousy both times. Come on, you look at guys and –

JOSH. I don't sleep with them.

RUBY. Never?

JOSH. No… It's okay, it doesn't matter. I should have said if I didn't want… (*Pause*.) Listen, I was thinking, next time you have a Mattachine meeting or whatever they call them do you want me to come with you?

RUBY. I ain't going back.

JOSH. Oh.

RUBY. Bunch of peacenik smart-ass college-boy anti-war… I went down there yesterday. I was telling them about how fucked up the whole military hang-up about queers is and all they can say is 'there shouldn't be queers in the army. We should be peaceful'. Just like that.

JOSH. You didn't tell me.

RUBY. It's not like I spend my days meeting people who say well done, Ruby, proud of you for fighting for your country.

JOSH. I am. I'm proud of you. For that. (*Pause*.) You signed up, you stuck it out. It counts.

RUBY. Thank you. At least you are. I got a discharge record says I can't ever get a decent job in the country I busted my ass for.

JOSH. I know. It sucks. (*Beat.*) Well. It's not like you're teacher material anyway. (*Pause.*) I slept with a guy in London.

RUBY. Really?

JOSH. Yeah.

RUBY. You slept with an English boy?

JOSH. Yeah. Well, he was Irish.

RUBY. You picked up in a bar? What are the bars like, are they amazing? I bet they're amazing.

JOSH. You could at least feign jealousy. (*Pause.*) He was working with me.

RUBY. Did people at work know he was queer?

JOSH. No. But I did. (*Pause.*) He was a nice guy, Ruby. I just… I dunno, it made me think. There are guys I meet out and about or at work – here in New York, I mean. And I know they're queer in the way that you just know, and sometimes I think it would be so easy. To meet someone who's like me and is queer but it's not everything to them and they just want to get on and make something of themselves like I do, and it would maybe be really nice to be with someone who wasn't intimidated by what I do and has to trash it all the time. And it would have to be a secret but it could work, it could be nice, you know? (*Pause.*) Sorry.

RUBY. Are you breaking up with me?

Pause.

JOSH. No. No, I. No.

RUBY. No like hell you are. Not here. You wanna break up with me, you take me to yours, you tell me there, you make me a drink and we stand on your balcony and you tell me there.

JOSH. I'm not.

RUBY. And I can shout and scream and make a scene and get every motherfucker staring out of their windows and up from the street, staring at this crazy dragged-up queen laying in to that young man they see sometimes, seems nice and bright and handsome but a little dull and a little shady. (*Pause.*) But not here. You're not leaving a shitty memory like that here where I get to come back to it every night with you back in your apartment, forgetting me like a bad dream. You can poison your own home. (*Pause.*) Why ain't you splitting up with me?

JOSH. Because I love you.

RUBY. I love you.

JOSH. Because you got to give things your best shot.

RUBY. Yeah. (*Beat.*) Wow.

JOSH. Yeah. (*Pause.*) I'm gonna take a shower.

RUBY. Can I do your back?

JOSH. Give me a minute.

    RUBY *kisses him.* JOSH *lets him.* JOSH *goes to exit.*

RUBY. It might be cold. The hot water's been playing up all week.

    JOSH *goes.* RUBY *looks out of the window. Turns back to the room, considers putting it into some sort of order. Doesn't know where to start. He follows* JOSH *into the bathroom.*

Scene Seven

The room above the bar. There is a small bed, and a small scruffy desk. FRANK *sits on the bed, in vest and underpants.* JIMMY *is naked, stood by the desk, he bends his nose to the desktop to snort a rough line of coke. He sniffs and gets back into the bed, lies back.*

JIMMY. You like that, mister?

FRANK. Yeah, weren't bad, kid.

    Pause.

JIMMY. Is this your office?

FRANK. Something like that.

JIMMY. Businessmen get to travel places, don't they. You get to travel?

FRANK. Not so much.

JIMMY. You could go to London, they changed the law there. You could open a joint. A real nice –

FRANK. What did you do to your shoulder?

JIMMY. Oh. (*Beat.*) My dad did that to my shoulder.

> *A beat.* JIMMY *sits up and points to his arm.*

And this is from when he put my arm through the window. (*Beat. He laughs.*) This I got from a cigarette setting my shirt on fire but I did that myself when I fell asleep in a doorway. (*Beat.*) I don't see them no more. Well, I saw my mom three weeks ago. Went home to see if there was food there, and my brother, cos I like my brother, but they don't like me being around my brother. I'm a 'bad kid'. (*Beat.*) I'm not, though. (*Pause.*) You can go back down to the bar now if you want. I'll let myself out.

FRANK. And leave you to go through my stuff?

> JIMMY *leans forward, putting his arms round* FRANK.

JIMMY. What do you take me for, mister?

> FRANK *laughs.* JIMMY *gets out of the bed.*

Fuck you.

FRANK. Get dressed. Then I'll pay you.

JIMMY. Cunt.

> JIMMY *starts to dress.*

FRANK. I could break your fucking legs for speaking to me like that. But I ain't going to. Know why? Cos I reckon you got balls. How do you fancy earning a few extra bucks?

> JIMMY *pauses dressing.*

I seen you. You're a bright kid.

JIMMY. You talkin' about fucking?

FRANK. No no no, shhh. Working for me. Making deliveries and stuff.

JIMMY. Neat! And helping in the bar?

FRANK. Maybe... What do you think?

JIMMY. Me? A job? Working with you? Me? Would I like to work here with you? You bet I would, Mr Frank. You bet I would.

Lights go down. They exit.

Scene Eight

ANGIE *is cleaning the bar. There is knocking from the front door. She ignores it.*

ANGIE. Morons.

The knocking changes to a pattern. ANGIE *laughs.*

(*Calls.*) Gimme a second.

She exits to open the door.

(*Offstage.*) Jesus, Rube, what happened?

ANGIE, JOSH *and* RUBY *enter.* RUBY*'s face is grazed and bleeding.*

JOSH. It looks worse than it is.

ANGIE. What you done now? Keep your blood off the floor, I just cleaned it.

RUBY. It's seen worse.

ANGIE. Do you want some water?

RUBY. No. Why? I'll have a whiskey. No one is speaking to me like that and getting away with it. No one!

ANGIE *gets water from behind the bar and a towel,* RUBY *starts to use it to clean the wound.*

ANGIE. Like what?

RUBY. Dirty fucking faggot. (*Beat.*) And he meant it in a bad way.

ANGIE. What, Josh?

RUBY. No! Some prick in –

JOSH. We were in a café, I went to the restroom, and Ruby decided to flirt with –

RUBY. I was talking with him.

JOSH. You said you flirted with him.

RUBY. I was talking with this guy at the table next to ours, passin' the time, and then his friend that he's waiting for walks in and suddenly he's embarrassed talking to me looking like this – *enjoying* talking to me – so he freaks out and calls me a dirty fucking faggot.

JOSH. So Ruby hit him.

ANGIE. Rube! What if he'd been a cop?

RUBY. I thought he *was* a cop. They try that shit.

ANGIE. So what happened.

RUBY. He and his scumbag friend start hitting me.

JOSH. Because you punched him.

RUBY. I stood up for my rights! You joined in.

JOSH. Of course I joined in. I came into the room and saw two meatheads laying into my boyfriend! You looked... you looked really little somehow. (*Beat.*) And they were losers, Ruby, who the fuck did they think they were.

ANGIE. You rescued him?

JOSH. I care about you, Ruby. The fact is, you got called a name. And now you have a broken face.

RUBY. It's not a name. It's who I am. I like me.

JOSH. There's liking yourself and respecting yourself. (*Pause*.) You don't have to dress like a fucking idiot queer all the time.

RUBY *slaps* JOSH.

Sorry.

RUBY. Last year, I got friendly with this beautiful kid from Ohio. I was totally in love with him and he idolised me for some reason. Completely hetero, married, the sweetest guy. Got his head blown off. (*Pause*.) Like you said, Josh, you only live once.

JIMMY *enters*.

JIMMY. What happened to you?

JOSH. He made a pass at Joe Frazier.

ANGIE. We're closed, honey.

JIMMY. Not to staff.

JOSH. Staff?

JIMMY. Yep. Mr Frank has made me head bartender.

RUBY. And I'm the Secretary of fucking State.

ANGIE. I'm head bartender. Frank!

JIMMY. Not any more. I'm in charge. And I want you to call me Miss Jimmy from now on.

ANGIE (*shouting*). Frank!

FRANK *enters*.

FRANK. You yelled?

ANGIE. Tweety Pie here reckons you gave him a job.

FRANK. Yeah I have.

JIMMY. See, told you.

FRANK. He's my assistant, aren't you, kid? What the hell happened to you?

ANGIE. No way, Frank.

FRANK. Guys, let me and the kid have a chat, huh. Ruby, clean yourself up in the restroom, Christ.

ANGIE, JOSH and RUBY exit.

JIMMY. You said I could work in the bar, Mr Frank.

FRANK. And you will, kid. But I need you to run some errands first.

He hands JIMMY a packet.

Deliver this for me. And just so you know, I know exactly what's in it and I want it to get there.

JIMMY. No problems, Mr Frank.

FRANK. Good boy. When you get back, come and see me upstairs, eh?

JIMMY. You said no more fucking.

FRANK. For me, kid. You're my special boy. Not like that other trash out there. Then maybe you can help in the bar.

FRANK ruffles JIMMY's hair and exits out back. JIMMY exits into the front lobby.

JIMMY (*offstage*). Hey guys, look at me. Yeah, you street kids out there. It's me, Miss Jimmy. Working here for Mr Frank.

He re-enters and crosses to the little stage, imagining himself as a singer. He sings a few lines of 'Fly Me to the Moon', badly.

DANNY enters.

DANNY. Why are you in here, kid?

JIMMY. I work here.

DANNY. That right.

JIMMY. I'm the deputy manager. Mr Frank asked me.

DANNY. Well, Mr Deputy Manager, is Angie here?

JIMMY. Could be.

DANNY. She in the back?

JIMMY. My staff are too busy to talk to you.

> DANNY *laughs*.

DANNY. Would you give this to her for me?

> DANNY *holds out a letter*.

JIMMY. Nope.

> DANNY *offers* JIMMY *a dollar bill*.

> I'll see she gets it.

> DANNY *loiters*.

> Something else you lookin' for?

DANNY. Is there something behind the bar for me?

JIMMY. We're closed. Officially. But I can get you a drink. You
want a drink?

DANNY. Don't worry, I'll call by again. What's your name, kid?

JIMMY. What's it to you?

DANNY. How old are you? You got family?

JIMMY. Yeah – no. Sort of.

DANNY. You don't need to be scared of me.

JIMMY. I ain't scared of you.

DANNY. Where do you live?

JIMMY. I live all over the place.

DANNY. You mean you got a load of houses or you mean you
live on the street?

JIMMY. Sometimes.

DANNY. Your parents kick you out?

JIMMY. No. I left.

DANNY. Why?

JIMMY. My mom ain't been sober since she had my brother
and my dad hits me.

DANNY. Sorry.

JIMMY. What the fuck do you care?

DANNY. That what made you queer?

JIMMY. Jesus, what is this, I don't fucking know.

DANNY. There are people who could help you.

JIMMY. I like being queer.

DANNY. I mean, to get along.

JIMMY. Sure there is. Maybe they'll train me up, huh? Maybe they'll train me up to be an astronaut!

DANNY. That what you wanna be?

JIMMY. I ain't stupid, Officer. (*Beat.*) And yeah course I would, who wouldn't. I even got the same name as Captain Kirk. Same first name.

DANNY. I love *Star Trek*.

JIMMY. *Lost in Space* is better.

DANNY. They stopped making it.

JIMMY. I didn't know that.

DANNY. I used to have a crush on Judy.

JIMMY. Are you the cop Angie went on a date with?

DANNY. Yeah.

JIMMY. You like her?

DANNY. It's complicated.

JIMMY. Why?

DANNY. You wouldn't – it's not as simple as do I like her.

JIMMY. Why?

DANNY. Different lives, different families… A bunch of stuff.

JIMMY. Captain Kirk kissed Lieutenant Uhura in *Star Trek* last year. They were different. One was black one was white.

DANNY. Half of America was up in arms.

JIMMY. The stupid half.

DANNY. Just because people get ideas it doesn't make them stupid. I think sometimes you need to have some rules that are a bit unfair to some people, just to make things work okay. I'm not explaining that so well. How old are you?

JIMMY. How old are you?

DANNY. Twenty-six.

JIMMY. Eighteen.

DANNY. Off the record.

JIMMY. Sixteen…

DANNY. Bet twenty-six sounds light years away, right?

JIMMY. It sounds like ten years. And light years is distance, not time.

DANNY. You got me. Well, to me, it feels like a minute ago that I was sixteen. You don't want to suddenly find you're twenty-six and some gangster like Ravelli. Listen, I got to go, Jimmy. I'm on duty. Mind if I drop by and chat again some time?

JIMMY. Why?

DANNY. Because you're a nice guy to talk to.

JIMMY. You can say if it's something else you want, you know.

DANNY. It's not.

JIMMY. You're weird.

DANNY. You're weird too. Nice to meet you… James?

JIMMY. Miss Jimmy.

DANNY. Nice to meet you, Jimmy. And my name's Danny.

He holds out his hand for JIMMY *to shake.* JIMMY *ignores it.*

JIMMY. And I said my name was Miss Jimmy.

DANNY. I'll come back for the, er... Tell Mr Ravelli I was expecting something. Miss Jimmy.

DANNY starts to exit.

JIMMY. Wait.

DANNY. Yep?

JIMMY walks over to him and holds out his hand. DANNY shakes it.

Look out for yourself, okay?

DANNY exits.

Scene Nine

The Baker's Tavern. A couple of days later. ANGIE's finishing giving the floor a quick mop. JIMMY is at the bar, reading one of the pamphlets. A record is playing on the record player. JIMMY occasionally sings the odd phrase along it. Badly.

ANGIE. See, the thing about records is, they already got singing on them.

JIMMY doesn't look up. ANGIE continues sweeping. JIMMY sings again.

They get real singers in to record them. With nice voices.

JIMMY. You're all sweaty.

ANGIE. Why thank you, what a gentleman, yes you may take over a while.

She offers him the mop. He ignores it.

Thought you wanted to work in a bar, you wanna do some work?

JIMMY. You ever sleep outside?

ANGIE. No. Why would I do that?

JIMMY. When it's hot like this it's nice.

ANGIE. Yeah?

JIMMY. And it's safer too because there's more people about. Wow.

ANGIE. What?

JIMMY. You got a really big ass.

ANGIE. Hey. At least it ain't my main source of income. Right... come on, gimme a hand here.

JIMMY. What's the magic word?

ANGIE. I dunno. Darvon?

JIMMY. Hah, yeah. No. I don't take that shit no more, it makes me sloopy.

ANGIE. Sloopy? Come on, do something.

JIMMY. I'm reading.

ANGIE. I told you, don't let Frank see you with that gay rights stuff.

JIMMY. I'm cool with Frank.

ANGIE. No, you're not.

JIMMY. Change the record.

ANGIE. You change the record, I'm cleaning.

JIMMY. It's an expression, dumb-ass.

ANGIE. I'll give you an expression.

JIMMY. Fat-ass.

ANGIE. I'm too hot to argue. Or clean. The place is a shit-heap anyway.

JIMMY. Then don't clean. You got a kid, yeah?

ANGIE. Why?

JIMMY. Just askin'.

ANGIE. I got a kid.

JIMMY. Cool! Can I babysit?

ANGIE (*faux-nice*). Why yes, Jimmy, that would be very NO, no you cannot babysit my kid.

JIMMY. Why not?

ANGIE *keeps cleaning*.

Why not?

ANGIE. I got a babysitter.

JIMMY. I'm good with kids.

ANGIE. Jimmy, you are a kid. What are you, twelve?

JIMMY. Fuck you.

ANGIE. Hey.

JIMMY. When I was younger, about ten and my brother was five, used to look after him all the time. Played with him. Got him food and stuff.

ANGIE. Yeah?

JIMMY. Yeah. (*Pause.*) We could take him on a day trip.

ANGIE. Your brother?

JIMMY. No, your kid. And my brother! We could pick up my brother, take him and your kid – what's his name?

ANGIE. Benjy.

JIMMY. Yeah, take a trip to Coney Island! No wait, he likes dinosaurs, we could go to that museum where they have dinosaur bones. Does – what's his name again?

ANGIE. Benjy.

JIMMY. Does he like dinosaurs?

ANGIE. He's three.

JIMMY. So tomorrow, let's go tomorrow. We can pretend we're married and – wait, that's stupid, Tommy's not young enough to be our kid.

ANGIE. Jimmy.

JIMMY. Huh.

ANGIE. Jimmy. No.

She goes off with the mop.

JIMMY. Are you mean like this at home? (*Shouts off.*) Poor fucking kid.

JIMMY *returns to his reading then remembers something.*

Hey. I forgot, there's some stupid letter for you.

ANGIE *comes back. She takes the letter from* JIMMY, *opens it, reads it. She's upset by it.*

ANGIE. Piece of shit.

JIMMY. What is it?

ANGIE. Seems I stupidly managed to talk someone out of something that might have been very nice. That's all.

JIMMY. This a love thing?

ANGIE *doesn't answer. She exits. He calls after her.*

He thinks you're too different.

JIMMY *reads for a moment.* RUBY *enters.* JIMMY *looks up, says nothing, carries on reading.*

RUBY. Well, hey, kid, how was school?

JIMMY. You're funny. Soldier girl.

RUBY. And?

JIMMY. Huh?

RUBY. Beautiful. I'm funny and beautiful.

JIMMY *ignores him.* RUBY *goes to the jukebox, puts a coin in, selects a track. Nothing happens. It doesn't return the coin.*

JIMMY. It ain't working.

RUBY. Then why didn't you tell me that, motherfucker? I just put a coin in.

JIMMY. We're saving for a new jukebox.

RUBY. Motherfucker!

ANGIE *returns*.

That piece of shit just swallowed my dime.

ANGIE. Jimmy?

RUBY. No. That piece of garbage. Jukebox. Jukebitch more like. Jimmy pockets the money and swallows the you-know-what.

JIMMY. Get more than a dime for it.

ANGIE. You should sing tonight. I haven't heard you sing since we opened.

RUBY. That's cos when I sing, you usually get raided. It's like I'm a mermaid, those cops just can't resist the sound of my voice.

ANGIE. Funny. I make them run a mile.

RUBY. What, girl?

ANGIE. Nothing. Danny. The cop. You were right about Benjy.

JOSH *enters, reading a letter*.

Josh, if that's more political crap.

JOSH. It's not.

ANGIE. Even the kid's reading the stuff now.

JIMMY. It's interesting.

RUBY. You can read?

JIMMY *shoots him a look*.

Last time I saw someone as skinny and mean and weird as you he jumped out of a jungle with slanty eyes and a machine gun.

JIMMY (*toying with him*). I never slept with a soldier before.

RUBY. I slept with plenty. (*Pause.*) And I ain't a soldier.

ANGIE. Josh, we ain't open.

JOSH. I got a letter from my father. (*Gives it to* RUBY.) See this bit.

RUBY *scans it, focuses*.

RUBY. 'Your mother and I would love to see photographs of your friends, especially the colourful-sounding Ruby. I am happy that you have found someone to make you happy, and proud of the hard work you are doing...' You told your father 'bout me?

JOSH. Sort of.

ANGIE. You thought to mention what's in his panties?

RUBY. You told him I'm your girlfriend! A photograph there shall be! They put their address on here?

JOSH. Don't. I owe my folks everything. They still pay for my apartment. Angie, do you think maybe you could be in a photo with me?

ANGIE. What? No! (*Beat*.) I ain't 'colourful'.

JIMMY. You ain't Twiggy neither.

RUBY. He was gonna ask you on a date last I heard.

ANGIE. What's he talking about?

JOSH. Nothing, it was stupid, I have to go to this fundraising dinner with work. It'll be very boring.

ANGIE. Like a ball?

JOSH. No. I mean they'll have a band but –

RUBY. I told him you'd hate it.

ANGIE. Yeah. I'd just hate a swanky dinner and a dance. Hell with it, I'm game.

JOSH. Oh. Really? I had to ask someone from work now. Sorry.

ANGIE. Thanks a bunch, Ruby. Well, there you go. No dinner, no photograph.

JOSH. Okay.

RUBY. Just tell them. I bet they know already.

JOSH. Do you ever think about what if your kid grows up gay, Angie?

ANGIE. Like I need another queer in my life. (*To* RUBY.) You gonna sing tonight?

FRANK *enters*.

RUBY. I think I might. Do you have... (*Whispers in her ear.*)

JIMMY. Money in the bowl.

RUBY. What?

JIMMY. If you request a record you gotta put money in the bowl.

RUBY. Since when?

FRANK. Since the jukebox broke.

RUBY. If I'm paying I want pretty lights.

FRANK. Angie, this is the rest of the money.

ANGIE *snatches it,* FRANK *exits*.

ANGIE. Anyone else wanna give me a fucking envelope today?

ANGIE *looks at the envelope, opens it, looks inside, closes it. She puts it in her pocket.*

I'll be back in time to open up. I'm sick of this fucking hole.

She exits out to the front and the street.

JOSH. You think I should see if she's alright?

RUBY. The cop let her go. She's better off without him.

JOSH. What are you gonna sing?

RUBY. W–A–S.

JIMMY. What's W–A–S?

JOSH. Wait And See. (*Beat.*) That's what Mom always said when I asked what was for dessert. W–A–S.

DANNY *enters*.

DANNY. Sorry to disturb.

RUBY. Go away. You upset my friend.

DANNY *doesn't look at him.*

DANNY. I just saw her... is she... Jimmy, did Frank leave anything for me yet?

JIMMY (*not sure what to say*). Not with me.

DANNY. Right... okay. Tell him he's an idiot, then. (*Goes.*)

RUBY. Prick.

JIMMY. He's okay.

RUBY *looks at him.*

RUBY. Go to your room.

Blackout.

Scene Ten

That night. The bar is open and lively. JOSH, JIMMY, ANGIE, RUBY *and* FRANK *are there.* RUBY *leans against the bar,* ANGIE *is rummaging through records.*

RUBY. You got it. There. Do I really have to put money in a fucking bowl?

ANGIE. This one's on the house.

She gets a record, puts it on the turntable, holds the needle poised.

RUBY (*to the crowd/audience*). Now, ladies and gentlemen. I know you can see I love my pretty clothes. But, well, I love to wear other things too. Way back when I was just a little soldier girl out in Vietnam, I... (*Mock-dramatic.*) well, I killed a man. God knows I didn't mean it to happen. Turned out it really was a gun in my pocket, and, as he lay there, bleeding attractively into the wet earth, I thought, my, what a fine pair of boots. My, I said, what a fine pair of boots. He looked up at me with forgiving eyes and said, Ruby, take them. I said, but surely, a soldier should be buried in his boots. And he looked up at me, and I couldn't help notice he still had an erection for me, how sweet I thought, and how strange it's always the little things one notices at a time like that. And with a last gasp he said, no girl, these boots, these boots were made for walking.

He sings over the record, a real performance. Suddenly we hear a hammering on the door, and the lights flash up, painfully bright.

Crap. Did it again.

FRANK. I'm outta here.

FRANK *exits out the back.*

JIMMY. Is this a raid?

ANGIE. It's a raid.

JIMMY. Cunts.

RUBY. That's the spirit.

A door is broken in. Something smashes.

JOSH. Angie, get me out of here. Please.

JIMMY. I'm a Village girl. And it's my bar. We gonna keep them out?

RUBY. Sure are. Come on, pigs. These fists were made for fighting.

Blackout.

Interval.

ACT TWO

Scene Eleven

A military base somewhere in the United States, autumn 1968. A room, windowless, underground. RUBY *is sat in a chair in his off-duty army wear. There is a table. Two* ARMY OFFICIALS *face him.*

OFFICIAL 1. Aw, look at this. A hero returns. Congratulations, Rudi, that's quite a military career, 1967 to 1968. Wow, huh? Glad to be back? Land of the free. (*Beat.*) All that shit.

RUBY. Where am I?

OFFICIAL 1. You're in trouble.

RUBY. Looks like the janitor's cupboard.

The other OFFICIAL *smacks* RUBY, *hard.*

OFFICIAL 1. You're tired. We can come back tomorrow.

RUBY. No wait.

OFFICIAL 1. No. Wait.

The OFFICIALS *exit. A door closes and locks.*

Blackout.

Scene Twelve

Lights up on the same.

OFFICIAL 1. People mouth off about military food but that meat loaf was something, wasn't it?

OFFICIAL 2. Sure was.

OFFICIAL 1. Those boys should get a medal. (*Pause.*) You know why you're here.

RUBY. I made a complaint.

OFFICIAL 1. No.

RUBY. Yes, I –

OFFICIAL 1. It's not why you're here.

RUBY. I made a complaint.

OFFICIAL 1. We know. You were attacked. Made to suck a few cocks or something.

RUBY. They tried to do more than that. And beat me up trying.

OFFICIAL 1. What did the chief say.

RUBY. He said, 'it don't make you gay'. I said maybe but it probably makes them gay. I got hit, fuck's sake. I was told there would be an investigation.

OFFICIAL 2. There was. They found out you like sucking cock.

RUBY. No shit, dumbfucks. They weren't meant to be investigating me.

OFFICIAL 1. The week before you'd been prancing about in a dress.

RUBY. For a show! It was for a show! Even the fucking general was there. In the front row. He danced with me, Jesus.

OFFICIAL 1. The general can do what he likes. Do you know why you're here?

RUBY. Cos I'm queer.

OFFICIAL 1. No.

RUBY. Well, Jesus, what??

OFFICIAL 1. Rudi. You're a bad soldier. You're volatile.

RUBY. Volatile, like what the fuck does that even –

OFFICIAL 2. Volatile means –

RUBY. Yeah alright thank you, professor, I know what volatile means.

OFFICIAL 2 *hits* RUBY.

Jesus.

OFFICIAL 1. You're dangerous.

RUBY. Bravest fucking man in the battalion.

OFFICIAL 1. Brave and reckless.

RUBY. The whole operation's reckless. I saved lives.

OFFICIAL 1. You cost lives. You were a danger to your corpsmen. Unreliable on a mission. (*Beat.*) Here's the thing, we're gonna discharge you. If we discharge you because you're a fuck-headed live wire, there isn't an attorney who wouldn't make out it was caused by you being in 'Nam in the first place. You'd get an honourable discharge. You'd get your pension. You'd get medical care. (*Pause.*) We could do that. Or we can discharge you for being a homosexual.

OFFICIAL 2. No pension. No healthcare. And a permanent record that means you'll never work as a state employee, never work with a respectable firm, nothing.

OFFICIAL 1. We're here to help you.

RUBY. So show me the way to the meat loaf.

OFFICIAL 2 *hits* RUBY.

OFFICIAL 1. We want names.

RUBY. What names?

OFFICIAL 1. Come on, Rudi. You're not the only queer in the army. You write down the names of everyone you can think of. And we'll think about what kind of discharge you get.

RUBY. You wouldn't have enough paper.

OFFICIAL 1. We got paper and all the time in the world.

RUBY. If you just wanna know who to get a blow job from –

OFFICIAL 2 *hits him*.

I ain't squealing.

OFFICIAL 1. We'll come back. Some time.

They exit. Blackout.

Scene Thirteen

Lights up on the same.

OFFICIAL 2. 12 Apostle Street.

RUBY. Yeah, so.

OFFICIAL 1. But you didn't grow up there.

RUBY. Folks moved there two years ago.

OFFICIAL 2. I like that address. 12 Apostle Street... Way the number and the name go together. Like twelve Apostles.

OFFICIAL 1. I think he gets it.

RUBY. My parents know I'm queer.

OFFICIAL 2. We don't give a shit about what your fucked-up family knows.

OFFICIAL 1. Your mother. School secretary. State employee. Easy to have a word with someone. Get her fired. Your father... (*Consults a piece of paper.*) Car mechanic. Guess in that case we'd...

OFFICIAL 2. Have someone torch his garage.

Pause.

OFFICIAL 1. Names.

Pause.

RUBY. If I write down all those names, you're gonna have to send the biggest boat you got to bring 'em back here. (*Pause.*) But I ain't gonna write down those names.

Blackout.

Scene Fourteen

June 1969. Greenwich Village. The morning after the raid that closed Act One.

The street, near The Baker's Tavern. Bright hot sunshine. JIMMY is sitting against a wall across the street from the bar. DANNY approaches.

DANNY. Jimmy.

JIMMY. Fuck you, Officer.

DANNY. Hey. Fine. Cool.

He goes to leave.

JIMMY. You got a smoke?

DANNY takes cigarettes from his pocket. Offers the packet. JIMMY takes two, puts one behind the ear, the other in his mouth. He looks at the packet again and takes that too, putting it in his pocket.

DANNY. You shouldn't be smoking, kid.

JIMMY. You deaf?

DANNY. Excuse me?

JIMMY. Are you deaf?

DANNY shrugs, lost.

Cos I thought I said 'fuck you, Officer' and you're still here and talking at me.

DANNY. You better hope I'm deaf, kid. You shouldn't be talking to me like that.

JIMMY. I had a job, mister, a job, first time in my life, I got a job, not just a lousy job either, I had prospects, man –

DANNY (*amused*). Prospects!

JIMMY. Don't laugh at me. And now you closed the place and I'm back to where I was and I got no job and no nothing.

DANNY. You got my smokes.

JIMMY. Were you there last night? I didn't see you.

DANNY. At the raid?

JIMMY. At the fucking ball game. Yeah, the raid.

DANNY. No. I was at the station. Kid, I told you, the bar's run by criminals. I told you not –

JIMMY. Do NOT tell me you told me so. (*Beat.*) You coulda closed it down before last night. Least then I wouldn'ta known no better but you didn't, cos you wanted the money they give you.

DANNY (*cautious*). Hey, not here.

JIMMY. It's only cos Frank was out and Angie didn't leave the money… So that's your fault too. They took Angie last night, you know? Pigs. And she got a kid at home an' everything.

DANNY. It ain't up to me if we raid. Just cos a lady's got a kid doesn't mean she's above the law.

JIMMY. No, you need to be a cop for that.

DANNY. We released her straight away. I had her released straight away.

JIMMY. Why? Cos you know her?

DANNY. She's just the bartender… You know, it's for the best. It's not good to get involved with people like that.

JIMMY. What, so I should go get a job at NASA? Or become a cop?

DANNY. Well.

JIMMY. Could I become a cop?

DANNY. Well... sure, yeah, you could. One day.

JIMMY. Bullshit. Don't wanna be a cop anyway.

DANNY. Jimmy, it's a system. Okay? People like the Mafia, they choose to be on the outside and if they do that they gonna get busted some day. It's a choice.

JIMMY. But what about people like me? What about the normal people in the bar. They got arrested and they was just drinking and dancing.

DANNY. The place isn't legal. They don't have to drink there.

JIMMY. What's not legal about it?

DANNY. It's not licensed. You gotta have a licence. And they're probably selling cheap watered-down drink but pretending it's brands.

JIMMY. Like when we fill up the bottles?

DANNY. You saw them do that?

JIMMY. I... Fuck that, mister.

DANNY. And it's probably a front for something. Drugs money. They probably set the whole place up on criminal money. Half the money they take probably doesn't go through the business, so they ain't paying their proper taxes.

JIMMY. So?

DANNY. So taxes... You don't know why taxes are important?

JIMMY. No.

DANNY. So they pay for schools, and the army, and welfare, and keeping the streets safe and clean...

JIMMY. And you.

DANNY. Yeah. And me. So we all put our money in a big pot...
it makes us a community I guess.

JIMMY. I know this guy, she –

DANNY. She?

JIMMY. This queen at the bar, she was in the army. He.
Whatever. Was in Vietnam. They threw him out for being a
faggot so they wouldn't have to give him a pension.

DANNY. You can't be homosexual in the army.

JIMMY. See? We ain't all one big community, some of us.
We're disenfranchised.

DANNY *laughs*.

Fuck you. What?

DANNY. You been reading something?

JIMMY. Maybe.

DANNY. Disenfranchised...?

JIMMY. Fuck you.

DANNY. I'm sorry, okay? I'm sorry you got a job serving
drinks and you don't have one now. It sucks.

JIMMY. I wasn't just a waiter.

DANNY. Kid, you were just a waiter. You think you were
gonna get promoted or something?!

JIMMY. I woulda! He gets me to run errands and stuff,
deliveries, you know? I'm gonna find Frank. He'll still have
something for me. He thinks I got talent.

DANNY. Good luck with that. He tends to disappear when the
heat's on... What kinda deliveries?

JIMMY. I dunno. Packets and stuff. Money I guess.

DANNY. Where to?

JIMMY. Places. Apartments. Bars. An office.

DANNY. You meet people?

JIMMY. I ain't squealing. If you wanna know, take me in and arrest me and ask me and gimme fuckin' breakfast too cos I hear the food's okay at the station. But I ain't –

DANNY. Do you meet people? When you run errands. I ain't asking names.

JIMMY. Yeah. Course.

DANNY. Shit, kid. You shouldn't be getting mixed up with these people. They're dangerous.

JIMMY. Dangerous? How?

DANNY. Dangerous bullet-through-the-back-of-the-head dangerous.

JIMMY. Frank ain't like that.

DANNY. If you mess up.

JIMMY. I ain't gonna mess up.

DANNY. You're talking to a cop in broad daylight, kid. (*Pause.*) Listen… A few years back, Frank's brother sent him to put some pressure on a guy, a bookie, who owed his brother a lot of money. He was meant to rough him up a bit. Only Frank got carried away. Broke the guy's neck. He lost his brother a lot of money doing that.

JIMMY. So if you know about it –

DANNY. No evidence. Least, not that we could use.

JIMMY. Why? (*Pause.*) He ain't gonna do that to me. I don't owe him nothing.

ANGIE *approaches*.

DANNY. Angie.

ANGIE. Don't talk to me.

DANNY. Let me explain, you got to understand it's difficult for me. (*Beat.*) I'm sorry. (*Beat.*) You said yourself. It ain't easy.

ANGIE. Yeah well, it's all roses for me, ain't it. Jimmy, let's go, there's something wrong with the drains round here.

DANNY. Must be my birthday I'm so popular today. Look after this one.

DANNY *goes*.

ANGIE. You look rough.

JIMMY. I drank a lot last night.

ANGIE. Where?

JIMMY. Hotel.

ANGIE. What?

JIMMY. After the raid this queen had some money, she rented a room and like six of us ended up there. Then someone nearly burnt the place down cos she made this dress outta the curtains and someone got a cigarette caught on it while she was dancing about and we all had to get out there pretty quick.

ANGIE. You slept?

JIMMY. Couple hours. In a doorway.

ANGIE. Quite a night. Come with me.

JIMMY. Where?

ANGIE. I had a call from Frank this morning. He said to find you, we gotta meet him in the bar in half an hour. He wanted to meet at mine but I said hell no. I ain't having Frank at my place.

JIMMY. The bar's closed. It's boarded up.

ANGIE. There's a way in the back.

JIMMY. So I still got a job? Where's your kid?

ANGIE. At his aunt's.

JIMMY. Can we get breakfast?

ANGIE. You're the boss. You buy me breakfast. I got no money.

JIMMY. We don't need money. We can steal it from the deli on the corner.

ANGIE. Steal it?

JIMMY. I'll teach you, come on. Or no wait we can go to the
pancake place.

ANGIE. I told you I got no –

JIMMY. We'll tip and run.

ANGIE. Tip and run?

JIMMY. Eat and leave. There's a corner they can't watch you.

ANGIE. Great. I'm gonna be arrested two days in a row.

JIMMY. Come on. I'm starving.

They go.

Scene Fifteen

*The Baker's Tavern, shortly afterwards the same morning. It's a
mess from the raid. FRANK is on the phone.*

FRANK. No, calm down, calm – sorry – I'm not raising my
voice I'm just as pissed about it as you are. No, Jesus, no, it
was just a raid and we were – we were prepared for it. Yes.
Made it look pretty above board... I don't know, we didn't
make a payment to the cops or something but – No, there's
no problem with money. We're a classy bar, well organised,
it was a mistake. A mistake that's all –

There is a banging from out back.

I am talking straight with – hold on, I gotta get the door.
Genovese said what? Aw, come on, that's not fair, why
would you think I'm a soft touch? Look, I gotta go, get the
door. Bye, Papa.

He disappears out the back and we hear:

(*Offstage.*) What the hell you doing here?

RUBY (*offstage*). It's not good business to talk to loyal
customers like that.

FRANK (*offstage*). What do you want?

RUBY (*offstage*). I dropped my purse in all the excitement last night.

They enter.

FRANK. That door's supposed to be a secret.

RUBY. Like your bourbon's supposed to be Jack Daniel's.

FRANK. Well, if we're gonna talk about appearances... So they let you out?

RUBY. Out? Out of what?

FRANK. Angie said you was banged up.

RUBY. No. But they locked Josh up... It's kinda funny actually.

FRANK. Who's Josh?

RUBY. My banker boy.

FRANK. Oh, him. Never liked him.

RUBY. Okay, well, sorry to disappoint you but it's not like they put him on death row...

FRANK. I got a meeting. When did you last see your purse?

RUBY. When did you last see your penis, fatman.

FRANK. Get out.

RUBY. Sorry. Can I get a drink?

FRANK. I ain't a waiter.

RUBY. Not a cute one.

FRANK. They took the drink last night.

RUBY. Cops?

FRANK. Mainly the cops. A few drag queens were helping themselves in the chaos too.

RUBY. Damn, I never thought of doing that. Man, there's gonna be some cops with sore heads today.

FRANK. Yeah, I don't really give a shit about their heads.

RUBY. After knocking back the liquid shit you serve. You got nothing?

FRANK. Jesus. There's more upstairs.

RUBY. You have an upstairs?

FRANK. Can I ask you something?

RUBY. Shoot. But please, not literally.

FRANK. If you could drink anywhere... Like if you could dance with other guys in any bar in town. Legit. Would you still come here?

RUBY. Hell no. (*Beat.*) I don't know. Yeah, probably. I mean, I could make the Stonewall my regular place and everyone knows that's better than here, right?

FRANK. They do?

RUBY. But I still come here.

FRANK. That's nice.

RUBY. Frank.

FRANK. Yeah?

RUBY. You'd be outta business in a second.

FRANK. Yeah. I know.

RUBY. You ain't a bar manager, it ain't in your blood. But you'd just... pursue your other avenues. Whatever the fuck they are. If you got any.

FRANK. I got avenues.

RUBY. More than rest of us got.

FRANK. I'm fuckin tree-lined.

FRANK *chuckles at his own joke.* RUBY *looks at him blankly.*

Guess I just... (*Beat.*) Go on, get your purse, get outta here.

RUBY. You just what?

FRANK. Kinda like runnin' this kinda place. That's all.

RUBY. You getting me that drink?

FRANK *fishes in his pocket, pulls out a key, gives it to* RUBY.

FRANK. Out the back. Left. Metal door. Go upstairs. There's some bottles in there.

RUBY. You serious? You letting me inside your secret lair?

FRANK (*amiably*). You're a man in a dress, Ruby. You got kicked out the army. You like a drink at eleven in the morning. You're the lowest of the low. You think I'm worried about you seeing anything?

RUBY. Ouch.

FRANK *gives him the key.* RUBY *goes to leave but there is more banging at the door.*

I'll get that, shall I?

FRANK. You sit.

FRANK *goes.*

ANGIE (*offstage*). It's me, Frank.

ANGIE *and* JIMMY *enter with* FRANK.

RUBY. Why look, it's Peter Paul and Mary.

ANGIE. What you doing here?

RUBY. But who gets to be Mary... Frank's sending me on a secret mission.

RUBY *exits.*

ANGIE. Frank, what you playing at?

FRANK. Christ, Angie, he's getting a drink, get off my back. (*Beat.*) Look at this place.

JIMMY. Ain't so bad.

ANGIE. It's a sunny day. I could be in the park with my boy. What's the plan?

FRANK. Angie, it's your fault, fucking up with the payment. That's when they raid. It's a game... You gotta keep the personal stuff out of it.

ANGIE. Says you.

FRANK. What's that supposed to mean?

ANGIE. Forget it. You ain't gonna listen anyway.

FRANK (*to* JIMMY). And what's with you? You look more wasted than normal, you look like you're on another planet.

ANGIE. He had a big night.

FRANK. Big night for us all, huh. Okay, here's what's happening.

RUBY *enters, clutching a bottle of champagne and a battered disco mirrorball.*

RUBY. Frank, you romantic old queen!

FRANK. Not the champagne, Jesus.

RUBY. Sorry, I already licked the bottle. (*Swigs.*) Guess your largesse ain't as big as your large ass. Aw, come on, I'm teasing, a girl gotta turn to something when her man's inside.

JIMMY. Why'd they have to lock up the hot one.

ANGIE. Yeah yeah, keep your voice down, the Dow Jones will start falling if folks find out.

RUBY. He'll be okay, won't he?

ANGIE. He's got brains, manners and hard cash... hey, yeah, he'll be okay.

FRANK. Ruby, shut up. Listen, here's the thing. I got some boys comin' down, sort this place up, arrange supplies, get those windows sorted, someone broke one in the panic, idiots. Jimmy.

JIMMY. Yes, Frank?

FRANK. Keep an eye on things.

ANGIE. What???

FRANK. I want this place to look good. We gonna make this the hottest little queer bar in Greenwich. I need a pair of gay eyes on it. A pair of young gay eyes. So listen, we're reopening five days from now.

RUBY. It takes five days to change a window and hang a shiny ball?

FRANK (*to* RUBY). You're not here. (*To* ANGIE *and* JIMMY.) So the wife, she's sick, okay, and I not been spendin' too much time with her so I said we'd go away a few days, me and her and the girl.

RUBY. What kinda sick?

FRANK. I dunno, sick. Ladies' stuff. So there's a place we used to –

RUBY. You ever worry about that?

FRANK. Excuse me?

RUBY. You ever worry like one day your wife's gonna suddenly feel an itch or something, you know, down there... and it won't go away so she's a bit scared and she goes to the doctor or calls the doctor or whatever way round you people do it and –

ANGIE. Ruby.

RUBY....and the doctor he says, lady, I hate to tell you this but you got something nasty and you sure as hell didn't catch it from eating bad seafood.

FRANK (*aggressive*). Can you believe this bastard? What are you saying about my fucking wife?

RUBY. Nothing, Frank. I'm talking about you.

FRANK. Jesus, why are you so antagonistic? You want me to bar you before it even reopens? Now just shut up. (*Takes a pen and paper from his pocket. Writes on it.*) Jimmy. That place three blocks down you went to deliver that last package? You remember how you get there?

JIMMY. Sure.

FRANK. Go give the boys a hand and bring them back here to get started, okay.

JIMMY (*a bit nervous*). So… like you want me to tell them what to do?

FRANK. Yeah. I'll tell them to listen. Be nice though.

JIMMY. Neat.

ANGIE. Can I go now?

There is a banging, this time from the front of the bar.

FRANK. It's like we're already the hottest joint round here today.

JIMMY. Is it the cops?

RUBY. Hell no, it's daytime. They'll be doing worthwhile stuff. Or jerking each other off in the weapon store.

The banging starts again.

FRANK. This is gonna make my ears bleed. Angie, would you mind?

ANGIE. No, why would I?

ANGIE *exits.*

RUBY. What we supposed to do now. Talk about the baseball?

JIMMY. Where you from, Ruby?

RUBY. What??

JIMMY. Your accent ain't New York.

FRANK. Cultural melting pot, this city.

They both look at FRANK *as though he's a bit mad.*

RUBY. Newport, Carolina.

JIMMY. You ever go back?

RUBY. Went back a month ago. My sister had a baby.

FRANK. Don't tell me, they asked you to be the fairy godmother.

RUBY. Yes.

JIMMY. You think I'll have a kid some day?

FRANK *laughs*.

What?

JOSH *enters from the back with* ANGIE. RUBY *goes to him*.

RUBY. Baby, they let you out! You okay?

JOSH. Like crap. What do you think?

FRANK. You, five minutes and you're out of here.

FRANK *exits*.

RUBY. I know, babe, I know what it's like being banged up in that place.

JOSH. I could handle the cell, but when I was being taken down I passed Mr Romero.

RUBY. I got this thing for Cesar Romero. Old but hot.

JOSH. Mr Romero, he's a lawyer. Must have been there on some business.

ANGIE. And the point is – ?

JOSH. He knows the Morgantees.

RUBY. Who hate the Capulets, I did this shit at school.

JIMMY. What are you talking about?

RUBY. Romeo Romeo... Romero Romero...

JOSH. Just shut up, Ruby, will you! I met Mr Romero a few times at the tennis club when I went there with Mr Leveridge, my boss. We met the Morgantees there.

RUBY. What a swelegant, elegant party that was.

JOSH. Romero's bound to tell Morganti. Fuck, I've called work already to say I'll be late in and Leveridge's secretary said that he wants to see me today. At four.

RUBY. They won't fire *you*.

JOSH. They can.

ANGIE. Say it was a mistake, you just happened to stroll into the place.

JIMMY. Like he just happened to have Ruby's tongue in his mouth?

RUBY. Babe, if it happens it happens. You and me we'll go off together. Off to see the world. Two drifters off to see the world.

JOSH. I'm not a drifter! (*Pause*.) I got to go. I need to sort myself out.

ANGIE (*to* JIMMY). Come on, kid, let's make a start on on this place.

JIMMY. Naw, this is good.

JOSH. I can't keep coming down here.

RUBY. The bar?

JOSH. The bar, the Village.

Pause.

RUBY. My place? Us? What? (*Beat*.) I love you.

JOSH. I know.

RUBY. I wasn't telling you, I was quoting you.

JOSH. I got to go. I'll call you later.

RUBY. I been cut off.

JOSH. It's not like you're hard to find.

JOSH *goes to exit. As he does:*

JIMMY. You'll be okay. You want me to walk you home?

JOSH. Best not, I think.

JOSH *exits.* ANGIE *approaches* RUBY.

ANGIE. He'll be back. Not like the asshole cop.

RUBY. Thought I ain't smelt shit in the air.

JIMMY. We seen him earlier. I told him he's a dick. And I took all his smokes. Fucker. He thinks they closed this place for good.

FRANK enters.

ANGIE. Okay, Jimmy. Come on.

JIMMY. He thought I was a fuckin' waitress or something but I set him straight. Told him I'd still have a job with Frank, turns out I was right.

RUBY (*to* ANGIE). Can we get out of here? My head hurts. Come for a walk.

ANGIE. You know me, Rube, at your service. Be back in five, Frank.

They go, RUBY *pausing to pick up the champagne.* FRANK *and* JIMMY *look at each other for a moment.*

JIMMY. You should be careful of that cop, Frank.

FRANK. What cop?

JIMMY. The one that's always coming in here. Danny.

FRANK. Is that who you were talking about? You been speaking with him?

JIMMY. He thinks you done stuff. He says you killed someone. But I know you wouldn't do that. Least unless you had a really good reason.

FRANK (*nods*). What did he ask you?

JIMMY. Nothin'. He just talks at me like he wants to be my dad or something. He's only twenty-six.

FRANK. He tell you his dick size too?

JIMMY. I don't think he's into that. He's a loser, he thinks I'm nobody, like I just mopped the floor a couple of times or something. He wouldn't believe me that I had a real job doing stuff for you. I know this place ain't legal but so what, it's just a bar, right? The cops don't give a shit. Anyway. Thought I should warn you.

FRANK. You did right, kid… You, er, you know where you're
going.

JIMMY. Sure. See you.

*JIMMY exits. FRANK is fretful, paces a bit, unsure what to
do. Then he picks up the phone and dials.*

FRANK. It's me again. Nothing's wrong. Well… it's probably
nothing. Listen, it's just I think Jimmy's been talking to a
cop and I don't know what – Jimmy. The kid who – Oh,
well, he's this kid. Off the street but bright, a bright boy,
really something… What do you mean, another one? No –
No it's – I sent him over to Sam's, they gonna get the place
back in shape – Yeah, it's a hell of a mess, they dismantled
the bar and everything – I know, but it's gotta look nice.
There's competition, you know? Yeah I know but just cos the
Stonewall's a dive – Who? Oh, Jimmy – No of course not,
come on, what do you take me for?… That's not necessary.
No, really. He's smart, he's… So what do you want me to
do?… Listen, Papa, I can't, it's not – Okay. Yes, okay… I
will – I'm heading out of town with Teresa but after that –
Okay… before I go – No I'll, I'll do it. I've sent him to
Sam's, I'll go there now – Yeah, I said… oh.

His father has hung up.

Fuck.

FRANK *stands still for a while.*

Fuck.

*He picks up the mirrorball then puts it back down. He goes
out the back, and the lights turn off with a click.*

Scene Sixteen

Afternoon. ANGIE*'s apartment.* ANGIE *and* RUBY *are on the bed smoking a joint. Chilled. After a moment:*

RUBY. You even meant to be here?

ANGIE. What are you talking about, Rube, it's my apartment.

RUBY. Ain't it the 'grand reopening' of The Baker's Tavern tonight?

ANGIE. You think I should be down there getting my gown on and going through the RSVPs?

RUBY (*singing*). RSVPECT find out what it means to me. (*Giggles.*)

ANGIE. Shuddup.

She starts laughing, then coughing on the smoke.

RUBY. Did you do it with the cop in this bed?

ANGIE. No.

RUBY. You did!! That's kinda hot.

ANGIE. No more dancing with the devil in the blue dress. Put a record on, Rube.

RUBY *looks at the record player.*

RUBY. I can't reach.

ANGIE. Please.

RUBY *gets up, puts a record on.*

You heard from Josh?

RUBY. Nope. (*Beat.*) You ain't the only ones from different planets.

ANGIE. Sorry. (*Beat.*) I thought you were kinda good together.

RUBY. Liar.

ANGIE. Where did you meet him?

RUBY. In the street.

ANGIE. Just like that. More romantic than the trucks, anyhow.

RUBY. I hate that shit.

ANGIE. But you pick up boys in the street.

RUBY. Ain't like my parents are gonna introduce me to someone at a society ball, is it? Meeting someone in the street it's a... buzz. It's a connection... Like finding a needle in a haystack. The trucks ain't. Or the parks. Call me old-fashioned but I like to see a face.

Pause.

ANGIE. You think he'll come back?

RUBY. Josh? (*Beat.*) Yeah. For a bit.

ANGIE. For a bit.

RUBY. Irony is, if it wasn't that we had to hide away in the Village, we'd never have met in the first place.

ANGIE. Planets colliding.

RUBY. I like that.

They lay in silence a while.

ANGIE. You think Frank would give me a reference?

RUBY. What kinda reference?

ANGIE. Was just thinkin'. It's probably stupid, I walked past this little coffee shop today and they had a notice in the window. Wanting staff. It was a nice place and only open daytimes and you know Benjy starts kindergarten soon... I thought, yeah, maybe I'd get a proper job, a nice little café.

RUBY. Be a civilian again.

ANGIE. Yeah. How do you get a job at Macy's?

RUBY. I don't think Frank's the kinda guy you want a reference from. You know what pisses me off?

ANGIE. Yeah, but run through the list again, I got time to kill.

A sound – something hitting the window.

RUBY. Hell was that?

Again, a coin or stone hitting the window. ANGIE *goes to it, looks out.*

ANGIE. Jesus. What do you want?

DANNY (*offstage*). Angie – Can I come up?

ANGIE. No, fuck you.

DANNY. I have to talk to you. It's important – please.

ANGIE. Where'd you go? (*To* RUBY.) Someone let him in.

RUBY. Who is it? Our next customer? You can read his palms, I'll blow him.

ANGIE. It's Danny.

RUBY. Son of a bitch.

There is knocking on the door. ANGIE *goes to get it.* RUBY *arranges himself to look as casual as possible with a joint between his lips.*

ANGIE *and* DANNY *enter.*

Good evening, Officer.

DANNY. I'm sorry, Angie. I, erm…

RUBY. You're getting married.

DANNY. It's the boy.

RUBY (*singing*). Mad about the boy…

DANNY. Can he leave us for a moment, please?

RUBY. Always knew you were one of us, Officer.

ANGIE. What is it?

DANNY. Jimmy's dead.

ANGIE. Oh God.

RUBY. Dead?

DANNY. I just identified him. He was pulled out of the river this morning.

RUBY. Another one bites the dust.

ANGIE. Oh my God.

RUBY. With a splash.

DANNY. A man on a barge saw him. He didn't drown, he was shot.

RUBY. That sucks. (*Beat.*) Understatement, sorry.

ANGIE. Frank.

DANNY. Yes. I think so. Do you think so?

ANGIE. The stupid, evil, coward bastard.

DANNY. A few days ago I tried to warn Jimmy about –

RUBY. That's probably why he's dead, you idiot.

DANNY. You guys letting him get mixed up with a violent criminal is why he's dead, you freak. (*Pause.*) Can you help me find his family?

ANGIE (*shrugs*). No. It's not like we keep employment records…

DANNY. Right. But you think Frank…

ANGIE. Maybe not him personally. He's away. (*Pause.*) I don't…

DANNY. Could you help me find out? Prove it?

ANGIE. Danny, I dunno, he's mixed up with some serious…! I got my boy to –

RUBY. Angie, it's bullshit. Sentimental crap.

DANNY. Hey.

RUBY. Oh, what. You're gonna investigate?

DANNY. We will.

RUBY. Right.

DANNY. I'll see to it.

RUBY. How you gonna make that happen?

DANNY *doesn't answer.*

What's different this time?

DANNY *doesn't answer.*

Motherfucker, I asked you –

DANNY. Angie, this could be your boy some day.

ANGIE. Don't you dare. Ugh, Jesus, Danny. (*Pause.*) It's been five days. He coulda got mixed up with anyone. He's – he was – kinda friendly I guess. But I think Frank knew you'd been talking to him. I think he heard that. But I don't know if Jimmy said anything to him. What stuff did he tell you?

DANNY. Not a lot. But he was boasting. He seemed to think Frank was someone you'd want to impress.

RUBY. Well, that's dumb. See this is why things gotta change! Proper change.

DANNY. Ruby, this isn't about being queer. It's about a kid who's been murdered.

RUBY. Join the fucking dots, Officer. (*Beat.*) Didn't you notice that when you do a raid these days, people get angry about it? This is the beginning of the end. We ain't talking years and years. I'm talking Jimmy's generation. They gonna be the first. Not just arm in arm in Christopher Street but hand in hand in Bloomingdale's at Christmas.

DANNY (*to* ANGIE). If I can pin this on Frank and there's something you can help prove, will you? If I made sure you'd be safe.

ANGIE. See what you find out.

DANNY. I'll be back. Don't go anywhere?

RUBY. I had a flight booked for –

DANNY. I was talking to Angie.

ANGIE. You got my number.

DANNY. I'll see myself out.

ANGIE. Sure. (*Beat*.) Good luck.

    DANNY *goes. Pause*.

RUBY. Nice to have visitors, anyway.

    Blackout.

Scene Seventeen

The flat above the bar. FRANK *sits at a little desk, working things out, papers and pen. His jacket is on the back of his chair.* DANNY *bursts in. Angry. A gun held out at* FRANK. DANNY *just keeps the gun on him, not sure yet what to say.* FRANK *opens a drawer, looks inside.*

FRANK. If you want cash I got nothing till we open. You boys turned the place upside down last week.

DANNY. You won't be opening. Stand up.

FRANK (*stays seated, indicates the room*). Go ahead. Whatever you're looking for. (*Pause*.) Your, how do you call it, scrupulous colleagues at the station won't thank you.

DANNY. Up!

FRANK (*stands up*). Come on, Officer, don't act naive. This ain't how the game works.

DANNY. It's not a game. I identified Jimmy's body today.

FRANK. I don't know a Jimmy.

DANNY. Couldn't you have just slept with him? Why'd you have to get him involved?

FRANK. Oh... The kid? Shit... He just, he helped out in the bar, couple times. For pocket money, you know? (*Beat*.) I didn't see him round here in a week. Where'd they find the poor bastard?

DANNY. Why'd you kill him?

FRANK. Officer, making accusations like that could get a man in trouble. You know how it is with these street kids, Officer. They're all off their heads on anything they can lay their hands on. They sleep out in the park. They'll go off with anyone who shows them a bit of cash or kindness. Tragic, but... Anything coulda happened to him.

DANNY. It did. He was shot from close range.

FRANK. Why are you concerned about some thieving kid? (*Teasing.*) I guess he was pretty...

DANNY. Yeah, and that's why he's dead, ain't it.

FRANK. Sentimental cop. Just my luck.

DANNY *looks about the room.*

DANNY. You even got a bed in here.

FRANK. You calling me a faggot?

DANNY. No, Frank. I'm calling you a murderer. And not for the first time.

FRANK Oh! That right? You gonna say you were there when the bookie died? You and your superiors in an illegal casino?

DANNY. I was twenty-one. They told me not to say anything.

FRANK *reaches into the open drawer and pulls out a gun, aims it at* DANNY. *A moment.*

(*Laughs.*) People know I'm here, Frank.

FRANK. So? (*Pause.*) Who?

DANNY. If you shoot a police officer, you're dead. Game over. Put the gun down or I will shoot you.

They face each other for a long moment. DANNY *steps forward.*

(*Shouts.*) PUT THE GUN DOWN NOW.

FRANK *drops the gun.*

FRANK. I'm just a – (*Beat.*) I got a wife and a daughter.

DANNY. I know. Mr Francis Ravelli. The family man from Queens.

FRANK. You know – Danny – if you arrest me, your career's over. You'll be investigating missing poodles till you get your pension.

DANNY. You're filth, Frank. The queers hate us for raiding their bars. But they're too stupid to see you're exploiting them. Shitty liquor, drugs... And where's the money end up?

FRANK. You get your share of it.

DANNY. And the money that gets laundered? Korea. The Viet Cong. Even straight over to Mr Brezhnev. That money's buying weapons for the Commies to use out there to kill American soldiers. Like my brother. You think the queers in your bar know that?

FRANK. They don't think about nothing beyond the next drink or the next line or the next lay. (*Beat.*) You're as up to your neck in it as I am.

DANNY. I ain't arresting you.

FRANK. Okay. (*Beat.*) You ain't gonna arrest me and you ain't gonna shoot me. So what you gonna do?

DANNY. When did I say I wasn't gonna shoot you?

FRANK. Jesus help me, I got a family.

DANNY. And Jimmy didn't. Okay, here's what I want you to do. I want you to leave.

FRANK. Huh?

DANNY. Leave the city. I want you to walk out of this room, out into that sunshine, and leave New York, and not ever come back.

FRANK. You're crazy.

DANNY. And never come back.

FRANK. If I leave I'm a dead man! I... I know stuff. They'll
find me... they'll kill me.

DANNY. They'll kill you if you stay. (*Pause.*) Here's the thing,
Frank. You was right to worry about Jimmy. He told me
everything.

FRANK. There's nothing to tell.

DANNY. People. Places. You're better connected than your
shabby suit and shitty bar would suggest. You know a man
named Salerno?

FRANK. No.

DANNY. Frank.

FRANK. Yeah, course I do.

DANNY. Tomorrow, Salerno's gonna get a message. About how
you trusted some kid you took a shine to. About all the
things that that kid told to a cop.

FRANK. Bullshit.

DANNY. I had a discreet talk with my chief. Turns out he's well
connected too. Did you know he and Salerno drink in the
same club?

FRANK. No one's gonna put their ass on the line for a dead kid.

DANNY. No one's putting their ass on the line. Nobody's gonna
know except Salerno and my chief.

A long pause.

FRANK. This is all I know. You know? We all need to make our
dough.

DANNY. But you're a criminal.

FRANK. Criminal... I'm a businessman too, and I ain't done no
more harm to nobody than half the businesses in America.
You don't need to talk to Salerno. I'll leave.

DANNY. It's too late. Get out.

FRANK. My jacket...

DANNY *indicates it with his gun.* FRANK *takes it from the chair. Puts it on. Goes to leave.*

I didn't kill him. (*Pause.*) You won't be sleeping so easy yourself, Officer.

DANNY. That's called being human, Frank.

FRANK *exits.*

DANNY *listens to* FRANK*'s footsteps as he goes. He sits on the bed and lets out a big sigh. He takes his wallet from his pocket and pulls out a slip of paper. Then he goes to the desk, picks up the phone, and dials the number written on the paper. Changes his mind, hangs up. And exits.*

Scene Eighteen

The Baker's Tavern. It is late, after 1 a.m. RUBY *and* ANGIE *are sat in the bar drinking* FRANK*'s champagne and playing cards. They have been here some time. A police siren is heard.* ANGIE *loses a hand of cards.*

ANGIE. Crap.

RUBY. It's practice. 'Nam.

ANGIE. It's cards, babe. It's luck.

RUBY *shuffles the cards.*

No more. What time is it? Must be gone midnight.

RUBY. Later than that.

ANGIE. And it's still baking hot. (*Pause.*) Where the hell is Frank? You think he knows Danny's after him?

RUBY. Dunno.

ANGIE. You think Frank woulda killed him?

Pause.

RUBY. We could just open up.

ANGIE. There's no one on the door or anything.

RUBY. I'll go on the door. (*Beat.*) Or go out. Must be some people about. (*Pause.*) You should get your kid back.

ANGIE. Benjy? What do you mean?

RUBY. You hardly see him.

ANGIE. I see him daytimes.

RUBY. Not much. Not today.

ANGIE. He's at Mary's. It's better for him, you know? He's got his cousins there and… it's just better.

RUBY. Only cos you let it be.

ANGIE. Leave it.

RUBY. I just –

ANGIE. Leave it. Why you suddenly taking an interest in me?

Another siren.

RUBY. I care about you, girlfriend. (*Beat.*) Betty's busy tonight. You think Frank's scared?

ANGIE. He's probably done a runner for a while. Nothing's gonna happen.

RUBY. I know. (*Beat.*) If it does though. If cop boy arrests him. You gonna talk?

ANGIE. They can't investigate Frank without asking questions about this place and the cops are too tied up in it. (*Pause.*) Fucking hell, Rube, he was sixteen. (*Beat.*) Yeah I'll talk. If it helps. (*Shakes the bottle.*) We're dry. Your turn.

She gives him the keys. RUBY *stands up. There is knocking at the front door.*

ANGIE *and* RUBY. Fuck off.

The knocking continues.

RUBY. See. We should open.

JOSH (*distant*). Angie, you there? Ruby?

RUBY. What the hell? Can I let him in?

    ANGIE *indicates yes*. RUBY *exits and returns with* JOSH.

JOSH. You running a casino now?

RUBY. Are you drunk?

JOSH. A little.

RUBY. What you doing here?

JOSH. I was… walking.

ANGIE. What, at – what time is it?

JOSH (*checks*). One thirty… it's one thirty.

RUBY. I ain't seen you in a week… what were you doing in the
    Village without –

JOSH. I wanted to… think… I took a walk in the Village / and
    then I got talking to a guy –

RUBY. a walk in the –

JOSH. – and we went back to his. Drank a little.

RUBY. Fucked a little?

JOSH. Yeah.

    RUBY *laughs. Stops laughing. Another siren.*

    Listen to me. I was leaving his apartment and I heard
    shouting and screaming, there were cop cars everywhere,
    couple of vans. This girl, lesbian, asked me for a smoke and
    she was telling me it's all kicking off at the Stonewall.

RUBY. A raid?

JOSH. But she'd been in there with her girlfriend when the cops
    came in and it was, you know, the usual, told everyone to
    line up, everyone dressed in guy clothes stand over here,
    everyone dressed in girl clothes over there. But nobody lined
    up. They refused.

RUBY. Oh my God, come on, let's get there.

JOSH. Wait, they started fighting the cops. So this girl ran out but the cops got her girlfriend and dragged her into the van but she was fighting all the way. There are a hundred people round there. They're all jeering at the police and the queens are playing it like they're on stage.

RUBY. Yes, yes, yes, go guys – go.

JOSH. She thinks they're going to torch the place. With the cops inside.

RUBY. So let's get there.

ANGIE. Ruby, you're on your ninth life or something, stay away.

RUBY. This is it, kids. This is the night when we show we ain't taking no more. The storm's been brewing a long time. Come on.

JOSH. I came to tell you something.

RUBY. Tell me later.

JOSH. The bank offered me a job in London.

RUBY. You just been to London.

JOSH. I'm going to live there.

ANGIE. They're getting rid of you?

JOSH. Promoting me.

RUBY. That what they called it.

JOSH. It's a big opportunity. They didn't find out about me getting arrested. My boss said something, he said he thought maybe – maybe I'd fit in there more. Enjoy it… I don't know but I think he meant…

RUBY. They're parachuting you out.

JOSH. Something like that.

More sirens are heard.

RUBY. For fuck's sake, let's get out of here and into the action.

ANGIE. We'll have a drink. Josh?

She grabs the keys and exits.

RUBY. That Irish boy must be real special.

JOSH. It's nothing to do with a boy.

RUBY. I'll come visit.

JOSH. Maybe.

RUBY. Maybe?

JOSH. You even know how much a ticket to London costs?

Pause.

RUBY. Okay. Stupid of me. (*Beat.*) Cos I'm just a thrift-store assistant. I ain't the right type of guy for you.

JOSH. It's not about the right type. I'm not like that. Ruby, you're not the right guy for me even if I was here. (*Pause.*) You're a lovable guy, Ruby, you're a lot of fun, you're –

RUBY. Fun.

JOSH. Funny and passionate and you are the most amazing fuck I have ever… And you are sweet and you are gentle but you could also hurt me. One way or another, you would hurt me, and I think you need to work out what you want for yourself before you can be there for someone else.

RUBY. I know what I want right now / and I'm –

JOSH. You only ever know what you want right now.

RUBY. This is a call to arms. I'm going to the Stonewall. (*Beat.*) Good to know I been in your thoughts. That you weren't too busy to do some thinking.

JOSH. That's what people do. Smart people.

RUBY. Was I in your thoughts when you were with that guy earlier?

JOSH. Yes.

RUBY. I'm outta here.

JOSH *is upset.*

You okay?

JOSH. Yeah. No. I'm sad. I'm drunk.

Pause.

RUBY. Angie's getting champagne – you want – ?

DANNY *enters from the front.*

JOSH. Hell, I gotta go.

DANNY. It's alright. Angie here?

RUBY. Yeah.

DANNY. There's a riot kicked off at the Stonewall. I got to go there but I wanted to see if things were okay here. If she was okay.

RUBY. Thought you was looking for Frank?

JOSH. Frank?

ANGIE *enters with a bottle of champagne.*

DANNY. Angie, keep this place locked up tonight.

ANGIE. It was. What's going on?

DANNY. There was a raid at Stonewall and it's gone crazy. You weren't home. I just wanted to see.

RUBY. We know there's a raid, Officer. And that's right where we're heading. Cos the world starts tonight, Officer. (*Swigs champagne from the bottle.*) The world starts tonight!

He gets up to go.

JOSH. Hold on, what's this about Frank?

ANGIE. He's gone AWOL.

DANNY. I found him.

ANGIE. You got him?

JOSH. What's he done?

DANNY. We ain't taken him in but I sent him away.

RUBY. Look at my surprised face.

DANNY. The chief won't investigate it. You know that. I told him to leave. For ever. It was the best thing I could do.

ANGIE. How the hell?

DANNY. Told him a pack of lies.

JOSH. Tell me what the hell's going on.

RUBY. Someone killed the kid that worked here.

JOSH. Jimmy?

RUBY. Yep.

JOSH. Frank killed Jimmy?

ANGIE. Someone.

JOSH. But he was just a street kid. (*Beat.*) Why?

RUBY. Because he was just a street kid.

JOSH. How?

DANNY. Shot and dumped in the Hudson.

JOSH. And you let Frank go.

DANNY. Nothing would have happened if I arrested him. This way he's gone for good.

JOSH. And when he murders another kid? But it won't be on your patch so that don't matter. And it'll probably be just another street kid so that won't matter either. There are men and women down at the Stonewall right now getting arrested for dancing and drinking in a bar that's got no licence. Ruby gets arrested once a month just for putting on a skirt or a bit of eyeliner. Frank murders someone and he's allowed to walk free!

DANNY. It's not like that –

JOSH. Have some moral courage, you ignorant piece of shit. You let him go. You fucking let Frank go! (*Beat.*) Did he pay you?

DANNY. You don't understand how it works.

JOSH *punches* DANNY *in the face.*

ANGIE. Josh! Danny –

RUBY. My hero. (*To* DANNY.) You just the first on the list tonight.

JOSH. Not having some cop telling me what I don't understand.

DANNY. You people make me sick. Look at you playing cards and drinking champagne.

RUBY. It ain't us killed Jimmy and it ain't us lets the guy who killed him walk.

DANNY. Get real. The country's fucked. And me, I'm sick of it and most of all I am sick of this.

He starts to leave.

ANGIE. What are you going to do?

DANNY. I don't know. I think I'm through with this crap.

ANGIE. What should I do with this place?

DANNY. Open a fucking hat shop.

He takes off his police hat and throws it to her.

Here's your first.

He exits. Pause.

JOSH. I hit a cop.

RUBY. Yeah you did, now come hit some more.

RUBY starts to leave. JOSH and ANGIE remain. RUBY turns around and looks at them. They do not move.

Come on.

JOSH. I can't get locked up again.

RUBY. Angie? (*Pause.*) Jesus, Angie – this is about the future, our future, Benjy's future and you just sit there. I got no time to wait for you pacifists. There's a fight to win and tonight we will fucking show Betty we ain't taking no more.

He exits.

JOSH. What you gonna do about this place?

ANGIE. Clean it and tomorrow start looking for a new job.

JOSH. Wanna walk out?

ANGIE. No.

JOSH. Give you a hand?

ANGIE. Nothing to do really. (*Beat.*) Thank you though.

JOSH. I'm tired. My head's starting to hurt.

ANGIE. Go home.

JOSH. Yeah.

He slips an arm around her waist and kisses her cheek.

Night, Angie.

ANGIE. Goodnight, Josh.

She offers him the bottle of champagne.

Congratulations.

JOSH *takes it.*

JOSH. Thank you.

He exits.

ANGIE *remains on stage. There are more sirens outside, chanting, the full sounds of the riot swell up.*

The End.

Timeline

1903   In New York the police conduct the first recorded raid on a gay bathhouse.

1910   Gay men in London begin to gather openly in public places such as coffee houses and tea shops.

1921   The UK's Criminal Law Amendment Act 1885 is amended to make 'sexual acts of gross indecency between women' illegal. Sexual acts between men had been illegal since 1885. Under the Act, men and women could be prosecuted for engaging in same-sex sexual activities.

1924   The Society for Human Rights is founded in Chicago. It is the first known gay rights organisation in the US.

1950   US military involvement in the Vietnam War begins. The level of US involvement increases until the late 1960s, and continues until 1973.

1951   The Mattachine Society, the first national gay rights organisation, is founded in the US.

1957   In the UK, the Wolfenden Report is published. It advises the government that homosexuality should not be illegal.

1962   Illinois becomes the first state to decriminalise homosexual acts between two adults in private.

1964   President Lyndon Johnson signs the Civil Rights Act, banning discrimination based on 'race, colour, religion, sex or national origin'.

1966   The Mattachine Society stage a 'sip-in' at Julius Bar in New York. They are challenging the New York State Liquor Authority who are prohibiting the sale of alcohol to gays.

1967   The Sexual Offences Act decriminalises sexual acts between two men over the age of twenty-one in England and Wales.

1969   The Stonewall riots: On Saturday 28 June, at 1.20 a.m., police raid the Stonewall Inn, a Mafia-owned gay bar in Greenwich Village, on the grounds that the bar's liquor bottles are bootlegged. Patrons spontaneously and untypically refuse to cooperate with the police, a non-cooperation that escalates into violence, rioting and demonstrations over several days. The riots transform the gay rights movement from one limited to a few activists to a widespread movement for equal rights.

The first British activist group, The Campaign for Homosexual Equality, is formed.

1970   The first gay liberation march is held in New York City.

The Gay Liberation Front is established at the London School of Economics. It is formed in response to debates that gay men and women in London are not happy with the way they are treated.

1972   London's first official gay pride rally is held with about 1,000 people marching. Its date, 1 July, was chosen as the nearest Saturday to the anniversary of the Stonewall riots.

1973   Harvey Milk runs for City Supervisor in San Francisco.

The American Psychiatric Association removes homosexuality from its list of mental disorders.

1974   Maureen Colquhoun comes out as the first lesbian MP for the Labour Party.

1976   Harvey Milk is appointed to the Board of Permit Appeals, making him the first openly gay City Commissioner in the United States.

1977   Activists in Miami pass a civil rights ordinance making sexual orientation discrimination illegal in Dade County.

Harvey Milk wins a seat as City Supervisor in San Francisco and is responsible for passing a stringent gay rights ordinance for the city.

1978   Harvey Milk is assassinated.

1979   About 75,000 participants march for rights for lesbian and gay people in Washington DC. It is the largest march for lesbian and gay rights to date.

1980   The Democrats issue a stance supporting gay rights at the National Democratic Convention.

Scotland decriminalises homosexual acts.

1982   Northern Ireland decriminalises homosexual acts.

Wisconsin becomes the first state to outlaw discrimination based on sexual orientation.

1988   Section 28 of the Local Government Act 1988 in the UK states that a local authority should not actively promote homosexuality, publish material that promotes homosexuality or promote the teaching in schools of the acceptability of homosexuality.

1992   The 'Don't Ask, Don't Tell' policy is implemented permitting gays to serve in the US army providing they did not take part in homosexual activity. It leads to the discharge of thousands of men and women in the armed forces.

2000   Vermont becomes the first state in the United States to recognise civil unions between gay and lesbian couples.

Gay and lesbian people are allowed to serve openly in the armed forces in the UK.

2003   The Sexual Orientation Regulations in the UK makes it illegal for employers to discriminate against people on grounds of their sexual orientation.

2004   Same-sex marriages become legal in Massachusetts, making it the first state to recognise same-sex marriages.

2007   The House of Representatives approves a bill ensuring equal rights in the workplace for lesbians, gay men and bisexuals.

2008   The Supreme Court of Connecticut rules that same-sex couples have the right to marry, making it the second state in the US to legalise same-sex marriage.

2010   President Obama officially repeals the 'Don't Ask, Don't Tell' policy.

2011   New York passes a law to legalise same-sex marriage.

2013   Hawaii becomes the fifteenth state to recognise same-sex marriage.

The Same-Sex Marriage Bill is passed in the UK allowing same-sex marriages to be performed from 29 March 2014.

India's Supreme Court recriminalises gay sex, four years after the anti-gay law was suspended.

2014   Dozens of gay men are reported to have been arrested in northern Nigeria as police begin to enforce new laws that criminalise gay marriage and the membership of gay rights organisations.

Roger Jean-Claude Mbede dies, unable to afford medical care, having allegedly suffered malnutrition and sexual assault during time in a Cameroon jail. He was imprisoned for sending a man a text message saying 'I am very much in love with you.'

Human Rights Watch publish a report about police extortion and torture of gay men in Kyrgyzstan. Police are reported to target gay men in gay clubs, parks, hotel rooms and on dating websites.

Uganda's President refuses to sign a bill that would punish gay people with life imprisonment but says gays and lesbians are 'sick people who need help'. He believes that the bill was passed illegally.

The Winter Olympics in Sochi, Russia, remain a focus for protest about the country's law banning 'homosexual propaganda'.

Homosexuality is illegal in seventy-six countries.

A Nick Hern Book

A Hard Rain first published in Great Britain in 2014 as a paperback original by Nick Hern Books Limited, The Glasshouse, 49a Goldhawk Road, London W12 8QP, in association with Above The Stag Theatre

Front cover: composite image, background photo of Christopher Street thanks to Landmarks Preservation Commission, NYC; young man image: ©iStock.com/rhphoto

Designed and typeset by Nick Hern Books, London
Printed in Great Britain by Mimeo Ltd, Huntingdon, Cambridgeshire PE29 6XX

A CIP catalogue record for this book is available from the British Library

ISBN   978 1 84842 396 1